Y0-BCQ-714

The Costs of Congestion

An Econometric Analysis of Wilderness Recreation

The Costs of Congestion

An Econometric Analysis of
Wilderness Recreation

Charles J. Cicchetti
*University of Wisconsin,
Madison*

V. Kerry Smith
*State University of New York
at Binghamton*

Ballinger Publishing Company ● Cambridge, Mass.
A Subsidiary of J.B. Lippincott Company

 This book is printed on recycled paper.

Copyright © 1976 by Ballinger Publishing Company. All rights reserved. No part of this publication may be reproduced, stored in a retrieval system, or transmitted in any form or by any means, electronic mechanical photocopy, recording or otherwise, without the prior written consent of the publisher.

International Standard Book Number: 0-88410-452-4

Library of Congress Catalog Card Number: 75-29261

Printed in the United States of America

Library of Congress Cataloging in Publication Data

Cicchetti, Charles J
   The costs of congestion.

   Includes bibliographies.
   1. Wilderness areas—Economic aspects—Mathematical models. 2. Outdoor recreation—Economic aspects—Mathematical models. I. Smith, Vincent Kerry, 1945-   joint author. II. Title.
QH75.C5   333.7'8   75-29261
ISBN 0-88410-452-4

Table of Contents

Acknowledgements

The collaborative effort that resulted in this book was initiated in the summer of 1971 as part of the research of the Natural Environments Program at Resources for the Future, Inc. John Krutilla had proposed and orchestrated an extensive program of research on the problems associated with the allocation and management of natural environments. He has contributed greatly to the formulation and implementation of this research, both through his firsthand knowledge of the activitiy and his own analysis, with Anthony Fisher, of the conceptual problems associated with the management of low-density recreational resources.

The study could never have been undertaken and completed without the advice, support, and assistance of Robert Lucas and George Stankey of the Intermountain Forest and Range Experiment Station of the United States Forest Service. Bob and George provided the sample and consulted on both the structuring of the questionnaire and the attributes of wilderness recreation. The study has benefited immeasurably from their efforts. Frequent discussions with A. Myrick Freeman III, Anthony Fisher, and Robert Haveman also contributed to the work. David Bradford and Joseph Seneca provided helpful comments on earlier drafts of this research. Thanks are also due Roger Betancourt, Gardner Brown, Oscar Burt, Mark Sharefkin, and Eugene Smolensky for careful and very constructive reviews of the entire manuscript.

Seminars at the University of California at Riverside, the University of Pittsburgh, the University of Wisconsin at Madison, and the State

University of New York at Binghamton have also been helpful to the form and presentation of our findings.

Our colleagues at Resources for the Future have commented extensively on the research, as well. Most especially, thanks are due Blair Bower, Allen Kneese, and Clifford Russell. We are grateful to Kerry and Kirk Krutilla, who helped us with what seemed an endless set of questionnaires and envelopes. Rita Gromacki and Netti Rathje eased our work with fine typing of early versions of the manuscript, and Eileen Sinchaski made "sense" of the final draft. Michana Atterbury and Sid Seamans helped us in the form of the material by editing the manuscript.

Finally we are most grateful to our wives, Pat and Pauline, and our children, Colleen and Charles, and Timothy for their continued patience and encouragement.

List of Figures

List of Tables

Chapter One

Congestion: Concepts and Implications

Increasing professional and popular attention is being devoted to a variety of externalities, including air and water pollution, and urban congestion. As Rothenberg [9] notes, traffic jams, airport crowding, and public transit overcrowding are all forms of social congestion. In each case we find individuals engaged in activities that require the services of some common resource. Before proceeding into further discussion of the problems associated with congestion, it is desirable to set out a common vocabulary and clarify what we mean by externalities and congestion.

Externalities occur when an economic agent engages in an activity that has a direct effect on the welfare or productivity of one or more other economic agents.[1] Under this framework we must clearly note the distinction between the *existence* of and the *economic significance* of an externality. This scheme views externalities as technological phenomena and separates from their existence the question of whether they impact resource allocation. If the agent must pay for the full marginal costs (or is compensated to the full marginal benefits) associated with his actions, then the externality nonetheless exists but does not affect resource allocation. Therefore it would not be considered to have economic significance in our framework. Certain resources have the characteristic of being able to transmit externalities. The airport, highway, or public park all serve to transmit externalities at certain levels of use. Simply stated, the activities of each individual using the particular facility will influence those of other users at certain total levels of use. Thus, the passenger

---

1. Dorfman [5] pp. 5–6.

departing on a late evening or midday flight will not inflict external effects on other users of the airport facilities. However, should he select a flight during peak traveling times and the capacity of the airport is reached or exceeded, then each additional user's actions will affect those present in the facility.

We are therefore saying something about the technical process of generating externalities. For certain activities involving the use of particular resources, such use may proceed without external effects up to a particular maximum level. After that level, externalities are transmitted from one agent to others. We designate this situation as one where congestion, as we use it herein, is present.

Congestion has particular relevance to those cases where consumption of a resource's services may involve some interaction with others. It is easiest to recount examples in which the direct effect of this interaction is time related. Traffic tieups on urban highways and delays in takeoffs and landings at airports during peak use periods are examples. In these cases, it is possible to use the time loss as a measure of quality deterioration of the service flow. That is, we can say we are paying the same price for a set of services that has deteriorated. Alternatively, should it be more convenient (as Becker's [1] work has suggested in a number of cases), we can say that the price of a given service flow is a function of money and time costs. So as the time required to engage in it increases, the full cost does, as well.

Unfortunately, there is a large array of problems in which it is not possible to relate the quality deterioration associated with congestion to some time dimension. Moreover, it seems that those activities whose demands appear to be growing at the fastest rates with income growth, education, and increased leisure time are the most susceptible to quality deterioration through congestion, and the least amenable to linking that quality loss to a corresponding time loss. Rather, the effects are more subtle and elusive. It may well be that the lifestyle associated with increasing wealth and its required interaction with people within a work environment places a premium on limiting the effects of these interactions in other activities. The reasons for the inadequacy of time-related measures of congestion are not important here. Rather, it is our objective to examine alternative means of accounting for the effects of congestion, and from this examination to develop a general framework for modeling and measuring the quantitative effects of congestion.

As we have noted, congestion externalities will be important to resource allocation when those who impose them are not required to pay for the full consequences of their actions. It may be that such charges are neither technically (due to transactions costs) nor institutionally feasible. Nonetheless, efficient resource allocation and management decisions require that these congestion effects be measured and accounted for. For example, consider the use of a park. If the park's manager seeks to maximize the benefits derived by the park's users, then he must recognize two opposing forces. On the one hand, additional users will add to the total benefits derived from the services provided by the park through the increases to the number of individuals enjoying its facilities. At the same time, the presence of additional users (subject to the limits technically defined by the capacity of the park) may interfere with the activities of some existing users, thereby imposing congestion costs. Thus a full accounting of the benefits derived from the use of the park will recognize these congestion effects as real losses in the benefits derived from the facility. To the economist, a tradeoff is involved between the additions to total benefits from more users versus the costs they impose on others. Those managerial actions based on some consideration of efficient resource allocation must ultimately incorporate consideration of this fundamental tradeoff.

To define the economic carrying capacity of a resource, such as the park, is an aggregate problem. However, to accomplish this objective we must begin at a disaggregate level to determine the implications of user interactions for the benefits each individual derives from his own activities. So before congestion costs can be adequately reflected in the management policies of a given facility, or in investment plans for numerous user facilities, it is necessary to identify the effects of user interactions at the most disaggregated level.

While the analysis we shall develop is general, our particular examples will be drawn from the problems associated with the allocation and management of recreational resources. In Chapter 2 we begin by reviewing, very briefly, several potential models of consumer behavior. Each approach is found to be capable of allowing for a general class of congestion effects. Moreover, each of these frameworks (as well as others we have not mentioned) will imply a general relationship between an individual's willingness to pay for the recreational services provided by a given area, and congestion. Unfortunately, economic theory does not serve to isolate the best measures of congestion's effects, nor does it provide specific functional forms for the relationship between willingness-to-pay and congestion. Rather, we start with a weak set of assumptions and derive some general results. The models considered do vary somewhat in the degree to which their assumptions restrict behavior. None is sufficiently restrictive to be observationally different from the others in the outcomes we might expect. Without specific assumptions on the form the individual's preference function and technical constriants, economic theory can provide only limited information on the appropriate form of the willingness to pay relation. In the present case, it provides a prediction of the sign of the effect of congestion on willingness to pay.

This discussion should not be construed as critical of the importance of economic theory for the problem at hand. On the contrary, even this general formulation of the problem serves to uncover a rather serious misrepresentation of congestion in many previous analyses. Apparently recognizing the parallel between quality deterioration and marginal costs of the service flow we noted in our discussion of time-related measures, these efforts have analyzed congestion effects by adding the marginal social costs (associated with congestion) to the aggregate marginal private costs. This adjusted cost schedule may be compared with marginal benefits to derive optimal use levels.

The analyses of congestion effects presented in Chapter 2 clearly indicates that congestion costs are dependent on the preferences of each individual. They are not technologically determined through cost-minimizing behavior as we conventionally assume of the marginal private cost schedule. While the final outcomes are the same, our ability to operationally measure congestion costs is impaired by failing to note that it is the benefit function that should be adjusted, and not the cost function. Therefore we shall measure congestion's effects on individual willingness to pay. In these terms the marginal cost of congestion is determined as the sum of the reductions in each individual's willingness-to-pay function, which occurs as a result of the increase in use of a given recreational facility.

In the empirical analysis we focus on low-density or wilderness recreation. These activities generally are meant to include hiking, camping (and associated fishing), and the viewing of wildlife and scenery in a pristine, undeveloped setting. Such forms of recreation necessarily require undeveloped land resources largely of the character mandated under the terms of the Wilderness Act of 1964. We should, however, emphasize that the analysis can be applied to a wide array of problems, and most especially those management and allocation problems associated with environmental resources.

It should also be noted that the problem of congestion in low density recreation is one of the more important issues facing the land-management agencies with jurisdiction over our federal low-density recrational areas. Both the U.S. Forest Service and the National Park Service have devoted increasing resources toward improving management in the presence of growing congestion at our low-density recreational areas. While currently available data are limited and somewhat out of date, several overall observations do provide some perspective on the problem. Use of the National Forest Wilderness areas over the twelve-year period 1947 to 1959 increased by more than 350 percent.[2] The most recent information appears to indicate some moderating of the rate of growth in the demand for low-density recreation. Nonetheless, these activities remain one of the fastest-growing recreational activities. Since the facilities necessary to engage in wilderness recreation are fixed and cannot be produced by man, congestion problems will be more important for these activities than for many other attractive recreational pastimes.

There is good reason to believe that this pattern of continued growth in the demand for low-density recreation will persist for the conceivable future. Cicchetti, Seneca, and Davidson's [3] analysis of outdoor recreation participation patterns indicates that remote camping (a low-density recreational activity) is income elastic.[3] With increasing income and education, as well as some increased need for solitude for personal regeneration (see [13] for discussion), rapid growth in the demand for wilderness recreation can be expected to persist.

The pressure of increased demands raises inevitable questions associated with the allocation of recreation resources. There are at present approximately eleven million acres of land within the National Wilderness System, and perhaps another fifty million acres suitable for inclusion in some form of preserved status. Two

2. Fisher and Krutilla [6] pp. 417–18.
3. Cicchetti, Seneca, and Davidson [3] pp. 142–43.

economic questions arise concerning these relatively pristine resources: (1) How can existing low-density recreational areas be managed most efficiently, considering both present and future use patterns? (2) What should be done with the suitable land not now preserved in the Wilderness System or preserved under the Wild and Scenic Rivers Act?

Land-management agencies and the courts, through the National Environmental Policy Act, have begun to address these issues. One recent example involving the Army Corps of Engineers' Trinity River Project, makes this point explicitly:

> The Court raises a question as to the procedures utilized for projecting future "usage" of these recreational areas, as they would appear to be unsupported by the record. For example, there appears too little or no basis for the method employed to obtain estimates of site visitation at an area in its "unimproved" state. Whereas the Corps apparently keeps accurate visitation records of users of existing Corps facilities, it is not inappropriate to inquire . . . who records the treks of individuals into the wilderness. Conclusions arrived at based upon a procedure weighted in favor of developmental type recreation facilities does not take into account the desires of those who may prefer natural recreation.[4]

Efficient resource allocation requires the allocation of wilderness resources to their highest valued use. We must recognize that this principle does not imply that the level of use itself is maximized, but rather that the net benefits associated with the use are maximized.

It is at this point that we must address the question of how one adequately accounts for congestion and the extent to which the existing literature devoted to estimating the demand for recreation can be tapped for insights. In such an assessment it is useful to refer to the taxonomy developed by Cicchetti, Fisher, and Smith [2]. Three approaches to modeling the demand for recreation were identified largely by the character of their respective data base and were designated as follows: (a) site-specific area; (b) population-specific; and (c) site-specific user models.

The first (site-specific area) encompasses the class of models designated travel-cost demand frameworks. Generally these studies are based on aggregate data for a given site on the number of visitors coming from each of a set or origin zones to the site during the full

4. *Sierra Club* vs *Froehlke* [10] pp. 1092–93.

season. The model maintains as a fundamental assumption that to acquire the services of the recreational area, users must transport themselves to it, and that the costs associated with doing this dominate any nominal user fees. In order for this framework to yield estimates of an identifiable demand function, a wide variety of additional assumptions must be made (and the empirical results from such models assessed in terms of the likelihood that these assumptions are reasonable). All of these requirements need not be enumerated here (see Smith [11]). Rather we shall focus on the ability of the model to be adapted to measure the costs of congestion. It is not difficult to realize that possibilities here are limited, if they exist at all. Available data are aggregated across both individuals and time of the season so that we cannot identify those users and their behavior during varying levels of total use of the site. While in principle it might be possible to collect information at intervals within a given season, we cannot identify the individual or type of experience received at such an aggregate level.

Thus it would seem logical to turn to individual-based surveys. Here the past research falls into two general categories, which we have previously defined population-specific and site-specific user surveys. In the first case, the data is collected for a representative sample of households in a given area (i.e., state, region, or country). The sample necessarily includes both individuals who engage in low-density recreation and those who do not. It records information on their participation patterns and their individual socioeconomic characteristics. To date, these surveys have had limited information on the sites where each individual traveled to engage in the activities. Without such information, direct assignment of congestion and estimation of the marginal effects is difficult. We have two problems. First, there is simply a data problem. For instance, precisely what kinds of experiences did each individual have on his various recreational trips? Can we determine on the basis of behavior patterns the individual marginal valuations of congestion? On the basis of presently existing surveys neither of these problems can be resolved satisfactorily. While one might select proxies for the first, the second requires more specific information on individual behavior. In terms of the Becker model of household production we need to sort out demand factors from production factors, and with the information presently available it has not been possible to isolate or identify the separate effects.

The second type of individual survey is what we have utilized here, because it appears most suitable to the problem at hand. It has consisted, in previous studies, of attitudinal surveys of the users of a given area. While these analyses are also subject to limitations, they do allow identification of the individual user and with our amended methodology control over his experience.

We have selected a specific site for our analysis, the Spanish Peaks Primitive Area in Montana. In the following chapters the factors that are important for the satisfaction derived from wilderness recreation will be empirically analyzed. Primary among these characteristics is the perceived level of solitude. Measurement of solitude is a difficult problem; and solitude must be precisely defined in this context. Most users engaged in wilderness recreation are not alone; rather, they participate with friends or family. Accordingly, disruptions to solitude refer to the interaction with individuals outside the party. Hereafter it is this concept of solitude that will be discussed, and *not* the desire to be completely alone. Stankey [12] has utilized the recorded number of encounters or meetings with other parties in camp and on the trail as an effective proxy for disruptions of solitude.

There are further difficulties associated with the definitions of encounters and the measurement of their effect on willingness to pay. In Chapter 3 a survey research strategy is developed, and the issues associated with individual revelation of preferences are reviewed. Chapter 4 presents the empirical results in the form of estimated individual willingness-to-pay functions. Two estimators have been used with a variety of functional specifications. The results suggest a strong association between the measures of solitude disruption and the revealed willingness-to-pay. They therefore confirm our casual presumtions about congestion.

In Chapter 5 the model is applied to a simplified statement of the management problem illustrating how the optimal level of use of the Spanish Peaks Area might be determined. In addition, a generalization of the Krutilla-Cicchetti model [7] for evaluating the benefits required in order to justify preservation of additional natural areas is developed. This generalization incorporates congestion and its associated reductions in willingness-to-pay into the valuation model.

For both case study applications, it is necessary to assume that the total use-encounter relationship is somehow known for the area. In the case of the amended Krutilla-Cicchetti model, a comprehensive sensitivity analysis is performed, examining the implications of alternative specifications of the model. Further research is necessary, however, to determine the character of this relationship.

It should be noted that the specific findings of this study are relevant only for the Spanish Peaks Primitive Area and its users and are limited by the small scale of the sample survey. The methodology is, however, quite general and can be applied to any congestion problem. Nonetheless, further applications will be necessary before the allocation of environmental resources among competing uses can be adequately planned. In Chapter 6 the findings and other issues associated with the management and allocation of existing and proposed low-density recreational areas are discussed.

REFERENCES

1. G.S. Becker, "A Theory of the Allocation of Time," *Economic Journal* (1965).

2. C.J. Cicchetti, A.C. Fisher, and V.K. Smith, "Economic Models and the Planning of Outdoor Recreation," *Operations Research* 21 (September/October 1973).

3. C.J. Cicchetti, J.J. Seneca and P. Davidson, *The Demand and Supply of Outdoor Recreation* (New Brunswick, N.J.: Bureau of Economic Research, 1969).

4. C.J. Cicchetti and V.K. Smith, "Interdependent Consumer Decisions: A Production Function Approach," *Austrian Economic Papers* 12 (December 1973).

5. R. Dorfman, "The Technical Basis for Decision Making," in *The Governance of Common Property Resources*, ed. E.T. Haefele (Baltimore: Johns Hopkins University Press, 1974).

6. A.C. Fisher and J.V. Krutilla, "Determination of Optimal Capacity of Resource-Based Recreation Facilities," *Natural Resources Journal* 12 (July 1972).

7. J.V. Krutilla and C.J. Cicchetti, "Evaluating Benefits of Environmental Resources with Special Applications to the Hells Canyon," *Natural Resources Journal* 12 (January 1972).

8. K. J. Lancaster, "A New Approach to Consumer Theory," *Journal of Political Economy* 74 (April 1966).

9. J. Rothenberg, "The Economics of Congestion and Pollution: An Integrated View," *American Economic Review* 60 (May 1970).

10. "Sierra Club vs. Froehlke," *Environmental Reporter* (Bureau of National Affairs), No. 46, March 16, 1973.

11. V.K. Smith, "The Estimation and Use of Models of the Demand for Outdoor Recreation," Appendix to *Assessing the Demand for Outdoor Recreation* (Washington, D.C.: National Academy of Sciences, 1975).

12. G.H. Stankey, "A Strategy for the Definition and Management of

Wilderness Quality," in *Natural Environments: Studies in Theoretical and Applied Analysis*, ed. J.V. Krutilla (Baltimore: Johns Hopkins University Press, 1972).

13. Committee on Demand for Outdoor Recreation, *Assessing the Demand for Outdoor Recreation* (Washington, D.C.: National Academy of Sciences, 1975).

Chapter Two

The Modeling of Individual Congestion Effects

Economists traditionally view congestion as a cost associated with waiting lines or queues at public facilities. Hence, a natural measure of the effects of congestion is the amount of time spent in waiting or the extra time required to engage in a particular activity. More generally, congestion affects the quality of a service flow, and the quality deterioration it causes may be evidenced in terms of time, accident rates, pleasure, litter, sunbathing area, ecological damage, available fish, and a host of other measures. Each of these factors will affect different individuals differently, yet the conventional approach to economic analysis of congestion-related problems is to suggest that time is the only relevant factor, and that it can be used to measure the divergence between the marginal private cost and the marginal social cost of providing an additional unit of the service in question.

A second problem associated with the existing economics literature is that the level of modeling is aggregated to the facility or site level. Haveman's [10] recent discussion of congestion effects provides a good example of the difficulty in applying such aggregate procedures to the measurement of congestion costs. Figure 2.1 contains a diagram similar to the one developed by Haveman. *TWP* relates total willingness to pay, aggregated over all users, for a particular service flow to the total use. *TC* relates total private cost to the total level of use. *TC* is assumed to be composed of the long-run time and travel costs involved to gain access to and make use of the facility.[1] Assume that as total use increases beyond K, the facility is no longer

1. Haveman [10] pp. 5–8.

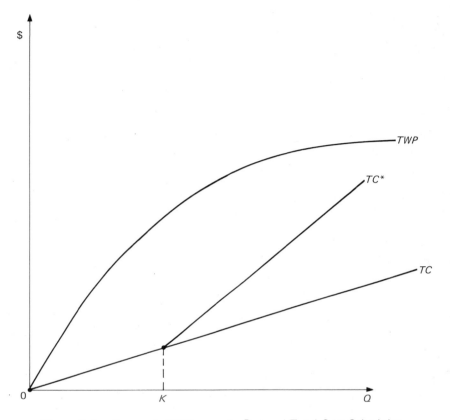

Figure 2-1. Aggregate Willingness-to-Pay and Total Cost Schedules.

capable of providing the same constant quality or homogeneous service flow to users. K defines the constant quality capacity of the facility. Hence congestion effects begin at the K level of use. Up to it, additional service units to new users do not impose negative congestion effects upon existing users.

Beyond the level of use K, the congestion costs may be added to TC to yield TC^*, which is the total social-cost function. Socially optimum policy requires maximizing the difference between TWP and TC^*. Conceptually, this approach is appealing and clear. However, its operational application requires a measure of the impact of congestion upon each individual user, and aggregation of these effects across all individuals, to provide the $TC^* - TC$ measure. This construction of the total congestion costs represented by $TC^* - TC$ measure is somewhat artificial. Congestion affects the real costs of obtaining a given service flow in a special way. That is, it changes the quality of the service flow reducing the satisfaction from the activities and therefore the individual's willingness-to-pay. It is the reduction in individual willingness-to-pay resulting from the perceived congestion effects of increased use that is the basic information necessary to measure aggregate congestion costs, $TC^* - TC$. Thus a disaggregate approach, based on a model of individual behavior, must be developed if applied analysis is to permit measurement and evaluation of congestion costs.

The purpose of this study is to develop willingness-to-pay functions that account for congestion effects, and to illustrate their use for solving problems. Investment decisions involving the allocation of environmental resources to amenity service production, and management decisions concerned with allocating fixed resources when congestion is present, are two such problems to be solved.

The first section of this chapter reviews several approaches for modeling the effects of congestion on individual behavior. It is followed by a discussion of the characteristics of wilderness recreation that previous empirical studies have found to be important to individual wilderness recreationists. The third section reviews the problems associated with soliciting individual willingness-to-pay information, and some recent experimental evidence. A 'final section summarizes the chapter.

ALTERNATIVE MODELS OF CONSUMER BEHAVIOR AND CONGESTION

As with many areas of applied economics, there are several observationally equivalent approaches for modeling the effects of congestion on individual behavior. None of the approaches offers a framework with explicitly testable hypotheses. Therefore, several alternative modeling approaches will be outlined and their implied relationship between individual willingness-to-pay and whatever congestion measure is germane to the model will be described.

The conventional approach to modeling individual behavior postulates that each person seeks to maximize utility subject to a budget constraint. Utility is specified as a function of the goods and services available. Generally, each commodity or service is assumed to be available in homogeneous units. The introduction of congestion and its impact on the quality of particular service flows implies a relaxation of this traditional assumption. Such a change does not, however, invalidate the conventional model. Rather, it extends the scope of the particular approach selected. One recent example is a model developed by Oakland [15], in which he examines the effects of congestion on Pareto-efficient resource allocations. In this model the consumer is assumed to select one private good and one public good. However, the public good is assumed to be subject to congestion effects associated with the level of total use of the services of a particular resource. Accordingly, the model specifies a congestion-cost argument in its utility function.

An alternative representation of the same phenomenon would call for a separate good in the utility function which measures the negative external effects of congestion, and can be presented as follows:

$$U^i = U^i (X^i_{Pu}, X^i_{Pr}, e^i) \tag{2-1}$$

where

X^i_{Pu} = amount of the public good consumed for the ith individual

X^i_{Pr} = amount of the private good consumed for the ith individual

e^i = external effect due to congestion for the ith individual

Given specific assumptions about how the public good is paid for and the relationship between (a) the external-effect measure and (b) the total level of use of the resource generating the public good, it is possible to derive the conditions describing individual behavior. The important point to be noted is that the model of individual behavior implies that the individual willingness-to-pay for the public good is related to: the amount of X_{Pu} consumed, the individual's ability-to-pay, and the amount of congestion the individual must endure (i.e., e^i).

Thus, individual willingness-to-pay for X_{Pu} can be specified as follows:

$$WP^i = f^i(X_{Pu}^i, Y^i, e^i, P_{X_{Pr}}) \qquad (2\text{--}2)$$

where

Y^i = income of the ith individual

WP^i = willingness-to-pay of the ith individual for X_{Pu}

$P_{X_{Pr}}$ = price of the private good, X_{Pr}

Equation (2.2) plus some additional assumptions concerning the partial effects of each determinant on the willingness-to-pay is not very explicit. If one is willing to specify a particular functional form for the utility function—relate e^i to the total level of use of the resource providing the public good—and thus further specify the model, in principle it is then possible to derive an exact functional relationship to replace Equation (2.2). A major drawback is that the outcome will be sensitive to the precise specification of the utility function as well as the use-intensity/congestion relationship. Accordingly, for applied analysis it is appropriate to suggest that Equation (2.2), along with the anticipated partial effects of each determinant of willingness-to-pay, are all that can be usefully derived from this particular line of reasoning.

A second theoretical approach might be termed the consumer-as-producer framework. Becker [2] introduced this framework; it assumes that individuals do not consume commodities, but, rather, use them in a household production process to generate consumption service flows that enter the individual's utility function. Under this analytical frame of reference, the services of a recreational area are demanded by the consumer because they can be used, together with time and other commodities, to produce a recreational service flow that directly provides utility.

Congestion can be specified as affecting the individual's ability to produce the recreational service flow. Consider a simple model in which there are three final service flows and four consumer inputs, specified as follows:

$$U^i = U^i(Z_1^i, Z_2^i, Z_3^i) \qquad (2\text{--}3)$$

$$Z_1^i = f_1(t_1^i, X_1^i) \qquad (2\text{--}4)$$

$$Z_2^i = f_2(t_2^i, X_2^i) \tag{2-5}$$

$$Z_3^i = f_3(t_3^i, X_3^i, S^i, e^i) \tag{2-6}$$

where:

$t_j^i =$ time of ith individual spent in jth activity ($t = t_1 + t_2 + t_3 + t_w$, where t_w = work time)

$X_j^i =$ amount of commodity X consumed by ith individual and allocated to jth production activity

$e^i =$ congestion effect experienced by ith individual in obtaining S

$Z_j^i =$ jth final service flow produced by ith individual

$S^i =$ quantity of site's services consumed by ith individual

Maximizing Equation (2.3) subject to production constraints, a budget constraint, and a time constraint yields a set of marginal conditions. If Z_3 is assumed to be the recreational final service flow, this maximization demonstrates that the derived demand for the quantity of services consumed, S^i, by individual i, is related to income, the prices of substitutes and complements (in production), and the amount of external congestion experienced. Accordingly, an individual's willingness-to-pay for the recreation trip can be analytically explained. Willingness-to-pay is one measure of the value of the recreation site's services to the individual, and it depends upon the congestion experienced. Therefore, this approach can also be used to derive empirical relationship.[2]

A third, and the final approach considered here, is to model

---

2. It should be noted that the problems raised by Pollack and Wachter [17] in the estimation of demand relations from the household production models are not relevant to our case. Pollack and Wachter note that constant returns to scale and absence of joint production are necessary if one is to hope to be able to estimate demand functions for the household's final service flows. While they do not express the issues in these terms, their arguments amount to conditions necessary to identify structural demand equations.

For our case, we are dealing with the demand for one of the inputs to this production process. Moreover we are not trying to infer these derived demands from behavior, but rather have them revealed directly by our respondents.

congestion using a model suggested by Lancaster [11, 12]. It assumes that

> consumption is an activity in which goods, singly or in combination, are inputs and in which the output is a collection of characteristics. Utility or preference orderings are assumed to rank collections of goods indirectly through the characteristics that they possess.[3]

One formalization of this model treats the individual as maximizing utility subject to a budget constraint, as in both the conventional and consumer-as-producer cases. With this framework, however, the utility function is a function of the attributes or characteristics of goods. These characteristics are a function of the goods, thus:

$$U^i = U^i(A_1, A_2, \ldots, A_k) \tag{2-7}$$

$$A_1 \leqslant g_1(X_1, \ldots, X_n)$$

$$A_2 \leqslant g_2(X_1, \ldots, X_n)$$

.
.
.

$$A_k \leqslant g_k(X_1, \ldots, X_n)$$

$$Y = \sum_{\ell=1}^{n} P_\ell X_\ell$$

and

$$X_\ell \geqslant 0 \text{ for all } \ell$$

$$A_j \geqslant 0 \text{ for all } j$$

The nonnegativity constraints upon goods (X_i) and attributes (A_j), and the inequality production relationships require the use of the Kuhn-Tucker conditions to analyze the first order conditions for a

3. Lancaster [11] pp. 133–34.

maximum.[4] Rewriting the objective function as in Equation (2–8), these conditions can be derived as shown in Equation (2–9):

$$G = U(A_1, A_2, \ldots, A_k) + \sum_{j=1}^{k} \lambda_j [g_j(X_1, \ldots, X_m) - A_j] \qquad (2\text{–}8)$$

$$+ \theta(Y - \sum_{\ell=1}^{n} P_\ell X_\ell)$$

where

Y = income
P_ℓ = price of X_ℓ

$$\lambda_j \frac{\partial g_j}{\partial X_\ell} - \theta P_\ell \leqslant 0 \text{ for all } \ell \text{ and } j \qquad (2\text{–}9a)$$

$$X_\ell [\lambda_j \frac{\partial g_j}{\partial X_\ell} - \theta P_i] = 0 \text{ for all } \ell \text{ and } j \qquad (2\text{–}9b)$$

$$g_j(X_1, \ldots, X_n) - A_j \geqslant 0 \text{ for all } j \qquad (2\text{–}9c)$$

$$\lambda_j [g_j(X_1, \ldots, X_n) - A_j] = 0 \text{ for all } j \qquad (2\text{–}9d)$$

$$Y - \sum_{\ell-1}^{n} P_\ell X_\ell = 0 \qquad (2\text{–}9e)$$

$$\lambda_j \geqslant 0, A_j \geqslant 0, X_\ell \geqslant 0 \text{ for all } \ell \text{ and } j \qquad (2\text{–}9f)$$

These conditions are similar to those derived from traditional analysis. The value (shadow price) of the jth attribute or characteristic is λ_j. Hence Equation (2–9a) suggests that the value of the marginal produce of the ith commodity in the production of the jth attribute must be less than or equal to its cost. Equations (2–9b) and (2–9d) allow for the possibility of corner solutions, and the other equations are subject to traditional interpretation. Each λ_j is a measure of the value the jth attribute. Congestion may be defined by the way it affects some of these attributes; hence, congestion cost will be a function of those λ_j's corresponding to the characteristics affected by congestion.

As in the previous two theoretical frameworks, the model can be

4. See Baumol [1] pp. 151–70 for a clear discussion of the Kuhn-Tucker conditions.

used to derive a relationship between willingness-to-pay and either direct or indirect measures of the congestion. Without more specific information on the utility function, consumers' production technology, or the characteristics-goods relationship, it is impossible to distinguish these models in terms of the testable hypotheses they imply.

In the first theoretical line of reasoning, congestion was directly entered into the utility function. But it differed from other goods and services in that it had a negative marginal utility. Under the consumer-as-producer framework, congestion entered one (or more) of the production functions. Individuals in their utility-maximizing decisions would equate the ratio of marginal utility products to price for each good. Congestion has a negative effect on the individual's ability to produce a homogeneous recreational service flow, that is, a negative marginal utility postulated in the conventional model.

As for the Lancaster model, a framework similar to the consumer-as-producer model was considered. Congestion affected the individual's ability to derive attributes from the service flow in question. It would reduce the quantity of a subset of the utility-producing attributes that are valued by the recreationist. Thus, while the attributes have positive values (measured by the λ_j's), congestion's marginal impact is to reduce them, and hence it has a negative effect on individual satisfaction.

Thus it is clear that each model renders the same general outcome, but by different mechanisms. While this consistency is reassuring, it is also disconcerting. Economic theory is not terribly useful for suggesting the appropriate form of the willingness-to-pay relationship. Instead it indicates what one already knew—that such a relationship exists. In conclusion, this theoretical review suggests that for applied analysis one does not need to dwell on the implications of the individual utility-maximizing behavior for the form of the willingness-to-pay relationship. Rather, it is possible to state that willingness-to-pay will be related to congestion, however measured.

In the empirical analysis that follows a specification is utilized which assumes willingness-to-pay to be related to the attributes or characteristics of the activity of central interest for our application—wilderness recreation. This specification was selected because it most naturally conforms with past research on wilderness recreation and individual preferences, primarily the work of Stankey [19]. As the previous discussion clearly states, it should not be construed as implying that this particular model is the only legitimate conceptual approach.

CHARACTERISTICS OF
WILDERNESS RECREATION

The preceding section suggests that there are several modeling approaches that can be used to derive a relationship between an individual's willingness-to-pay for a wilderness experience and either the attributes of that experience or measures of reductions to them due to congestion. Hence, specific effects of changes in one or more of these attributes upon this willingness-to-pay should, in principle, be measurable. To do so it is necessary to specify the attributes of wilderness recreation that are (a) important to the satisfaction derived from these experiences; and (b) affected by the total use of a particular facility.

The recreational services furnished by wilderness facilities are generally such that the primary interation sought is with the natural environment. Solitude has been found to be one of the most important attributes of these low-density recreational activities. This characteristic is, however, somewhat elusive, and there may be reason to suspect it means different things to different individuals. In 1969 Stankey [19] surveyed the users of four wilderness areas: the Bob Marshall Wilderness in Montana; the Bridger Wilderness in Wyoming; the High Uintas Primitive Area in Utah; and the Boundary Waters Canoe Area in Minnesota. Of all the users in his sample, 82 percent felt that "solitude—not seeing many other people except those in your own party," was desirable.[5] Moreover Stankey's results suggest that encounters with other parties may be an operational means of measuring disruptions of solitude so defined.

While it is true that the impact depends upon the type of parties met, and where they are met, in empirical applications a disaggregated measure of such meetings seemed to perform reasonably well as an indicator of a diminution of solitude.[6] A multivariate statistical analysis of these same data suggests that the reaction to crowdedness does vary with the individual. Using Stankey's data, Cicchetti [5] found that "the visitor who is older when he first visits a wilderness,

5. Stankey [19] pp. 100–101.
6. Ibid., p. 106–108.

who has had considerable auto camping and hiking experiences as a child, who has a discriminating view of the wilderness, and who did not grow up in a small town is the one likely to be most upset by congestion."[7] Such reasoning suggests a hypothesis that encounters are an effective measure of the reductions to solitude associated with increased use of a given wilderness facility at a particular time and place. Accordingly, it can be further hypothesized that encounters will affect an individual's willingness-to-pay for wilderness recreation.

There are a number of other characteristics of a wilderness area that might also be hypothesized as affecting an individual's willingness-to-pay. However, as discussed in the next chapter, the empirical analysis undertaken in this application is confined to a single wilderness area. Furthermore, setting aside congestion-related costs, increased use (at levels below the ecological carrying capacity) does not affect any of the inherent beauty of the scenery, flora, and so on; therefore, these attributes will not vary across individuals or their experiences in a given area.

It should also be noted that encounters may reflect more than disruptions of solitude. The individual may find certain other conditions, such as litter on trails or at campsites, reduce the feeling of solitude. It was not generally possible in this case study to separate these other effects on a characteristic-by-characteristic basis. But one potentially important distinction has been made in our analysis. Stankey has suggested that one should distinguish at the very least between trail encounters and encounters at a campsite. The reason for this is that each form of encounter may have different effects on the attributes of wilderness recreation and 'therefore on willingness-to-pay.

THE MEASUREMENT OF INDIVIDUAL
WILLINGNESS-TO-PAY

The preceding discussion ignored any problems that might be associated with measuring an individual's willingness-to-pay. But it is precisely because of distrust in the ability to measure individual preferences for such nonmarketed commodities as wilderness recreation that indirect approaches for the measurement of willingness-to-pay have been developed. In the case of outdoor recreation, the

---

7. Cicchetti [5] pp. 157–58.

Clawson-Knetsch [7] travel-cost approach for estimating the demand for outdoor recreation has been particularly noteworthy. The reasoning underlying this approach is that travel costs are likely to be the largest component of the "price" individuals must pay for recreational services. One drawback is that it is not generally possible for the travel-cost approach to control for the quality of each individual's experience. Therefore, the impact of congestion upon an individual's willingness-to-pay is not measurable using this method.

Our research strategy is different from the indirect empirical approaches. It consists of questioning wilderness users directly to obtain their willingness-to-pay for hypothetical experiences. This approach is not, however, without its potential problems. Samuelson [18] has discussed the problems associated with the revelation of preferences and noted that "it is in the selfish interest of each person to give *false* signals to pretend to have less interest" when he feels that he will have to pay for the good or service according to his revelations.[8] Equally important, if the individual believes that his answers will not be used as a basis of pricing, there may be incentives for him to overstate his enjoyment so that more and perhaps a higher quality of the good or service will be provided.

More recently Bohm [3] has expressed an alternative view. He suggests that:

> Once it is clear that there is no open-and-shut case for the individual when considering under- or overstatement of his preferences, the choice of strategy may well seem so complicated to him that he prefers to state his true maximum willingness to pay. Only an actual test of alternative approaches to estimating the demand for public goods could reveal the true state of affairs in this respect. But one important argument in favor of the hypothesis that people will abstain from the complicated calculations of optimal strategy inherent in our approach is that most people simply won't find such calculations worthwhile considering the small individual sums usually involved.[9]

In a series of follow-up experiments, Bohm [4] examined five approaches for determining willingness-to-pay for public goods. The schemes of interest range from, at one extreme, soliciting individual willingness-to-pay with knowledge that payments will then be based upon the response, to the other extreme of soliciting the same

8. Samuelson [18] p. 389.
9. Bohm [3] pp. 59–60.

information without tying payments to them. Bohm's findings indicate that none of the approaches (each applied to a random sample of consumers) exhibited a significantly different average maximum willingness-to-pay.

The approach used in this case study corresponds to one of Bohm's extreme cases in that each respondent was assured that his revealed maximum willingness-to-pay would not be used to alter existing pricing practices. While Bohm's findings would seem to indicate that our method does not provide significantly different responses from those of several alternative approaches, there remains no definitive assurance that the revealed willingness-to-pay reflects the actual level of satisfaction of each individual respondent. However, as indicated earlier, the primary interest of this case study is with the change in the level of willingness-to-pay in response to congestion, rather than the overall level of willingness-to-pay for wilderness recreation. Hence the absolute level can be biased, and the primary objectives attained, if individual respondents react honestly to the changes in attributes hypothesized and if the respondent sample is sufficiently large. So even discounting Bohm's results, the traditional nonrevelation problem may not be as serious for this study as it may be for others.

SUMMARY AND CONCLUSIONS

The rationale underlying the specification of individual willingness-to-pay functions has been developed. Additionally, those attributes of wilderness recreation that are affected by congestion have been discussed. Several observations deserve repetition.

1. The conventional approach for analyzing the optimum use of a public facility includes both congestion effects and private costs. While analytically convenient, operational measurements of congestion costs require that reactions to total use be assessed on an individual basis. Such valuations are most easily registered in terms of the diminished willingness-to-pay associated with congestion.
2. Integration of congestion into a model of consumer behavior can be readily accomplished by using several modeling approaches for consumer behavior. They include: (a) the conventional economic model, where a congestion effect directly enters the individual utility function; (b) the consumer-as-producer model, where

congestion affects the individual's ability to produce final service flows; and (c) the Lancaster model, in which consumers desire characteristics *associated* with goods rather than the goods themselves. Additionally, there is a technical relationship between goods and characteristics. Congestion is assumed to have an effect on the extent to which some service or goods can provide specific attributes.

3. The most important attribute of wilderness recreation is solitude. It will be defined as freedom from encounters with other parties. Stankey's results suggest that intrusions upon solitude (as measured by encounters with other parties) adversely affect the percent of his sample of wilderness users that indicate they would be satisfied with their wilderness experiences.

4. It is possible to derive an individual willingness-to-pay function and to relate it to the attributes of low-density recreational service flows, and to identify the specific attributes affected by congestion. Nonetheless, there remains the problem of measuring willingness-to-pay. Conventional wisdom suggests that there will be inherent biases in any attempt to directly solicit expressions of willingness-to-pay; but recent empirical evidence presented by Bohm indicates that there are no significant biases in the maximum willingness-to-pay revealed even under conditions that we would suspect to have such biases. Moreover, the principal purpose of the subsequent analysis is to measure how willingness-to-pay is affected by changes in the attributes measuring congestion. The analysis presented below attempts to measure the differential price effects of congestion, and it is for this reason that potential biases in the absolute level are less important.

REFERENCES

1. W.J. Baumol, *Economic Theory and Operations Analysis*, 3rd ed. (Englewood Cliffs, N.J.: Prentice-Hall, Inc., 1972).

2. G.S. Becker, "A Theory of the Allocation of Time," *Economic Journal* (September 1965).

3. P. Bohm, "An Approach to the Problem of Estimating Demand for Public Goods," *Swedish Journal of Economics* 73 (March 1971).

4. ____, "Estimating Demand for Public Goods: An Experiment," *European Economic Review* 3 (June 1972).

5. C.J. Cicchetti, "A Multivariate Statistical Analysis of Wilderness Users," in *Natural Environments: Studies in Theoretical and Applied Analysis*, ed. J.V. Krutilla (Baltimore: Johns Hopkins University Press, 1972).

6. ____, and V.K. Smith, "Interdependent Consumer Decision: A Production Function Approach," *Australian Economic Papers* 12 (December 1973).

7. M. Clawson and J.L. Knetsch, *Economics of Outdoor Recreation* (Baltimore: Johns Hopkins University Press, 1966).

8. A.C. Fisher and J.V. Krutilla, "Determination of Optimal Capacity of Resource-Based Recreation Facilities," *Natural Resources Journal* 12 (July 1972).

9. R. Gronau, *The Value of Time in Passenger Transportation: The Demand for Air Travel* (New York: Columbia University Press, 1970).

10. R.H. Haveman, "Common Property, Congestion and Environmental Pollution," *Quarterly Journal of Economics* 87 (May 1973).

11. K.J. Lancaster, "A New Approach to Consumer Theory," *Journal of Political Economy* 74 (April 1966).

12. ____, *Consumer Demand: A New Approach* (New York: Columbia University Press, 1971).

13. D. Nichols, E. Smolensky, and N. Tideman, "Discrimination by Waiting Time in Merit Goods," *American Economic Review* 61 (June 1971).

14. H. Nikaido, *Introduction to Sets and Mappings in Modern Economics* (Amsterdam: North Holland, 1972).

15. W.H. Oakland, "Congestion, Public Goods and Welfare," *Journal of Public Economics* 1 (November 1972).

16. J.D. Owen, "The Demand for Leisure," *Journal of Political Economy* 79 (January/February 1971).

17. R.A. Pollak and M.L. Wachter, "The Relevance of the Household Production Function and its Implications for the Allocation of Time," *Journal of Political Economy* 83 (April 1975).

18. P.A. Samuelson, "The Pure Theory of Public Expenditures," *Review of Economics and Statistics* 36 (November 1954).

19. G.H. Stankey, "A Strategy for the Definition and Management of Wilderness Quality," in *Natural Environments: Studies in Theoretical and Applied Analysis*, ed. J.V. Krutilla (Baltimore: Johns Hopkins University Press, 1972).

Chapter Three

The Role of Experimental Design and Econometric Methods for Estimating Congestion Costs

Each of the modeling approaches dealing with the impact of congestion on individual behavior has suggested that congestion be included in an individual consumer's willingness-to-pay function.[1] Accordingly, the empirical analysis discussed below will focus on the problems associated with estimating such relationships. The Spanish Peaks Primitive Area in Montana is the specific site, which will be the frame of reference for the sample of recreationists analyzed.

The principal objective is to measure the determinants of a "representative" individual's willingness-to-pay for a wilderness recreation experience at the Spanish Peaks Primitive Area. In particular, the effects of alternative perceived congestion patterns on this willingness-to-pay will be analyzed. In order to do so, it is necessary to specify the form of this willingness-to-pay relationship. Additionally, both the method of estimation and the design of the sample survey are not independent of the specification selected. These matters will be considered in the remainder of this chapter.

Economic theory, as noted above in Chapter 2, provides only general guidelines for the specification of an individual willingness-to-pay relationship. The specific arguments of the function will depend upon which of the approaches one selects for modeling individual

1. An individual's willingness-to-pay function specifies the price that individual would pay for each quantity and quality of a given good or service. It is therefore a quality-adjusted individual demand function, and the horizontal aggregation of these functions across individuals would be equivalent to the market demand. For the particular case under study, wilderness experiences do not exchange in organized markets, so that price data cannot be used to determine the demand relationship. Moreover our analysis focus on the demand for a single trip at the individual level.

choice. However, these determinants can be generally classified into three categories: (a) factors describing the individual's ability-to-pay, both in terms of income and the time available for wilderness trips; (b) variables describing the wilderness trip itself, including measures of congestion; and (c) measures of the individual's demographic characteristics as indicators of his or her taste for wilderness recreation.

Some of the characteristics of a wilderness trip can be assumed invariant across the individuals in our survey. These factors are related to the attributes of wilderness recreation that are area-specific, and therefore remain unaffected by the level of use of the area. Since we focus on the users of a single resource, it is appropriate to assume that the beauty of the scenery, flora and fauna, and so on, are invariant over the sample respondents. This specification greatly reduces the number of determinants of willingness-to-pay.

There is a second simplification, which is also important for the specification of the model, and it is related to the congestion measure selected. The measures utilized below are restricted to those developed by Stankey [13]. As noted above he attempted to gauge individual reactions to alternative configurations of conditions (or attributes) during a wilderness trip. His primary measure of disruptions-to-solitude—encounters—might function as a congestion measure in any of the three models described in Chapter 2. By restricting the analysis to the encounter-based congestion measures, the estimation will be simplified.

The estimation problem can be considered as one of approximating the willingness-to-pay function by a low-order polynominal in some defined region for the independent or explanatory variables. Those variables that may account for the differences in response across individuals are specified and analyzed. The problem of selecting values for the design factors to estimate this willingness-to-pay relation is treated within the general framework of estimating a response surface.

In addition to the above estimation questions, the cross-sectional character of the survey data and the potential need for a generalized least-squares method of estimation must be addressed. The first section examines the specification of willingness-to-pay functions. As already noted, economic theory does not offer concrete guidelines on either the form of the function or the measures of the experience that are important to users. Hence, experience with user-response data must supplement economic theory. In the second section the assumptions of the classical linear model are reviewed, the problem of experimental design and its implications for the survey research methodology are examined, and the econometric methods used are discussed. The third section briefly discusses the response pattern to the questionnaire and attachments used, and a final section summarizes the chapter. Appendix A at the end of the book presents the questionnaire materials.

THE SPECIFICATION OF WILLINGNESS-TO-PAY FUNCTIONS

An operational approach for the measurement of individual congestion costs requires, as noted, the definition of an individual's willingness-to-pay function (WP_i) in terms of the following variables: (a) physical measures of congestion; (b) the quantity consumed; (c) the individual's income and time resources; and—since all individuals are not alike—(d) demographic variables that reflect the effect of differing tastes for wilderness experiences.

In general, wilderness recreation is likely to have few perfect substitutes. But a wilderness trip to the Spanish Peaks Primitive Area may have a number of substitutes in terms of experiences at other wilderness areas. However, it is impossible to gauge exactly what activities and which areas will function as substitutes, and the extent to which each recreationist at the Spanish Peaks considers them to be substitutes. For practical purposes it is necessary to' assume that wilderness-area substitution effects are not important. Accordingly, Equation (3–1) provides a general functional specification of individual willingness-to-pay.

$$WP_i = f(q_i, Y_i, t_i, T_{1i}, \ldots, T_{ni}, C_i) \qquad (3-1)$$

where:

q_i = quantity of wilderness recreation taken by the ith individual

Y_i = income of the ith individual

t_i = time measures constraining the ith individual

$T_{1i}, \ldots, T_{ni}$ = taste measures for a ith individual

C_i = measure or measures of the congestion perceived by the ith individual

As noted in Chapter 2, Stankey's [12, 13] research suggests a more specific statement of the character of the congestion (C) measure. His surveys of wilderness users indicate that solitude is one of the primary attributes of low-density recreation, and that the effects of congestion on it can be measured by encounters. Moreover, the effect of each additional encounter with another party on an individual's satisfaction depends on the total number of encounters the individual has experienced. In particular, Stankey's research indicates that these encounters have a diminishing marginal effect.

One specification for the willingness-to-pay function that would accommodate this diminishing marginal effect is a semilog function in which the logarithm of individual willingness-to-pay is specified to be a linear function of the attributes of the wilderness experience and the socioeconomic characteristics of the individual respondent.

Figure 3.1 illustrates the effects of an increase in encounters upon willingness to pay under a linear and a semilog functional form. In the linear case (3.1a), an increase in encounters has the same dollar impact at each level of individual use, q_i. However, with the semilog specification (3.1b), the encounter variable is specified to have the same percentage effect. Thus, as the level of WP declines, so does the absolute magnitude of the effect. In terms of the diagrams, the impact for the linear case is AC at all levels of q_i in Figure 3–1a, and the absolute magnitude declines from EF at q_0 to GH at q_1 with the semilog form in Figure 3–1b.

As noted in Chapter 2 and in the preceding discussion, encounters with other parties will be used as the measure of intrusions upon solitude. Accordingly, the greater the number of encounters in a given trip, the less solitude experienced during it. This tentative hypothesis is simple enough, but its simplicity may obscure some important aspects of the problem. Both the kind of party encountered and the location of their meeting may also be important. Moreover, it is not difficult to envision the experienced wilderness recreationist as having anticipated the number, type, and location of encounters before taking the trip. That is, the actual experience relative to the expected experience may be a fundamental

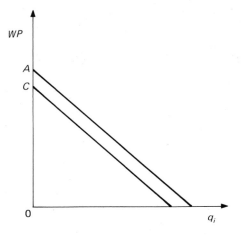

Figure 3–1a. Congestion Effects with Linear *WP* Schedules.

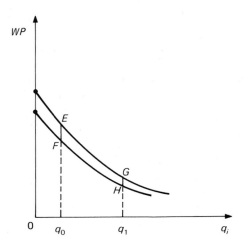

Figure 3–1b. Congestion Effects with Nonlinear *WP* Schedules.

determinant of perceived congestion, satisfaction, and, therefore, willingness to pay. Within this framework it might be postulated that the recreationist perceives congestion only when the actual experience provided (that is, the number and types of encounters) exceeds anticipations. If this model accurately describes behavior, and adaptive-expectations or partial-adjustment model would provide a reasonable approach to modeling.[2] However, the extent to which the resultant form of the willingness-to-pay function would be observationally different from that utilized in this study depends, in large part, on how individuals from their expectations.

Nonetheless, isolating the effects of different types of encounters upon willingness-to-pay is an important extension of the initial formulation. Moreover, the potentially different effects resulting from trail and camp encounters occurring with horseback parties versus hiking parties will also be studied. Further refinements, including the separation of periphery encounters (such as those occurring on the trails in close proximity to the entry point or trail head) from interior encounters, may be important; but our refinements are restricted to the inclusion of variables for trail and camp encounters and the examination of the effect of the encountered party's mode of travel on the estimated willingness-to-pay function.

THE GENERAL LINEAR MODEL AND EXPERIMENTAL DESIGN

Either a linear or a semilog specification can be legitimately considered, since they both serve as approximations of an unknown underlying relationship. From the perspective of estimation and

---

2. The adaptive-expectations model of this behavior would suggest that an individual's willingness-to-pay in period t is a function of the expected number of encounters, say E_t^* in that period. Thus, $WP = \alpha + \beta E_t^* + U$. If we suggest that E_t^* adjusts by comparing past expectations with the realized values of the variable, i.e., $E_t^* - E_{t-1}^* = (1 - \theta)(E_t - E_{t-1}^*)$, where $0 \leqslant \theta < 1$), then expectations become a geometric lag function of past experience. That is, $E_t^* = (1 - \theta)(E_t + \theta E_{t-1} + \theta^2 E_{t-2} + .. +)$. Alternatively we might postulate E_t^* to be a function of the previous period's experience (E_{t-1}) as well as the individual's knowledge of wilderness recreation and his socioeconomic characteristics. In this case, our specification for the willingness-to-pay function would resemble more closely the form we have used. In order to use the adaptive-expectations model we would require additional information from our respondents on their past experiences. This information is likely to be both difficult to obtain and subject to large errors.

experimental design, it is convenient that each description of individual willingness-to-pay is linear in the parameters. Thus, discussion of the problems of estimation may be confined to linear models for two cases, one in which the regressand— willingness-to-pay—is expressed in linear form, and the other with it in logarithmic form. For simplicity, the following linear model expressed in equation (3–2) can be considered for both cases:

$$y = X\beta + U \qquad (3\text{--}2)$$

where:

$y = TX1$ vector of values for the willingness-to-pay (or transformations of it)

$X = TXK$ matrix of values for the K regressors

$\beta = KX1$ vector of coefficients

$U = TX1$ vector of stochastic disturbances

The conventional assumptions of the general linear model are given in Equation (3–3) where u_i is the ith element in U, and x_i is the ith row of X.

$$E(u_i) = 0 \text{ for all } i \qquad (3\text{--}3a)$$

$$E(u_i^2) = \sigma^2 \text{ for all } i \qquad (3\text{--}3b)$$

$$E(u_i u_s) = E(u_i) E(u_s) \text{ for all } s \neq i \qquad (3\text{--}3c)$$

$$E(u_i x_i) = 0 \text{ for all } i \qquad (3\text{--}3d)$$

$$X \text{ is of rank } K \text{ and bounded variation} \qquad (3\text{--}3e)$$

These assumptions allow the ordinary least-squares estimator (hereafter OLS) of β to be the best of the class of linear unbiased estimators. Moreover, given $u_t \sim N(0, \sigma^2)$, the OLS estimates of β will also be normally distributed, and the tests of classical inference available for hypothesis-testing will be valid.

The OLS technique is derived from a quadratic-loss function as in Equation (3–4). With the normality assumption, the estimator that minimizes this loss function is also the maximum-likelihood estimator for the model.

$$G = (y^T - \beta^T X^T) (y - X\beta) \qquad (3\text{–}4)$$

Hence there are a number of good reasons for selecting OLS as the estimator for models that are linear in parameters and that can be assumed to have well-behaved errors.[3]

The extent to which these assumptions are satisfied is largely a function of the specific source of the data and the sample. Economists must usually accept data as published for use in their analyses. These data are collected by government agencies or tabulated from administrative data designed to serve nonresearch functions. Thus, unlike the experimentally oriented scientists, the economist generally does not have the ability to design experiments and collect data from them to test hypotheses. In social science research, reliance must be placed upon the data that is available, and the frequent use of proxy variables is characteristic of most empirical work in economics.[4]

There is, however, a growing body of literature on experimental economics in which it has been suggested that controlled experiments can be designed to test the effects of specific economic policies on the behavior of individuals and, more broadly, on the behavior of actual economic systems.[5] Most of these efforts have dealt with the effects of a guaranteed annual income. However, some additional work has been done with educational vouchers and housing allowances. These cases are distinguished from most research conditions in economics in that the analyst has the ability to control the character of his data (that is, the values for his independent variables—X in terms of the notation of Equation (3–2)).

The particular problem considered here is different from both past work with experimental economics and most empirical research in

3. See Theil [14] and Johnston [6] for more detail on these assumptions.
4. See Wickens [16].
5. See Naylor [8] for a review of some of the efforts with experimental economics.

economics. In order to measure the effects of congestion as reflected by encounters on wilderness recreation, it is necessary to have sufficient variation in the experiences of the sample respondents. Since the sample is based on the recreationists at the Spanish Peaks Area during one season, it is unlikely that their actual experiences, or rather their recollections of them, would be useful, since they would not exhibit sufficient coverage of the sample space of possible experiences. Accordingly, in the survey utilized in this study, a set of hypothetical experiences has been used. Additional details on this survey will be explained below.

Conventional empirical research in economics does not, as a result of the nature of its data, address the problem of experimental design.[6] The selection of observations with particular sets of values for the independent variables, so as to optimize some objective function with a recognition of the constraints implied by the problems at hand, is the problem of experimental design. When survey research has a specific objective, such as the estimation of individual willingness-to-pay functions, then the question asked should be tailored so as to improve the estimation of the desired relationship.

There are some important differences between objectives to the experimental design utilized in previous studies and that of the present study. First, in previous studies, the values of most of the independent variables were outside the direct control of the experimentor, since these variables were largely the economic and demographic characteristics of the individuals in the sample. However, through selective sampling it was possible to control the mix of individuals with particular characteristics. Moreover, these studies were generally interested in the effects of alternative monetary incentives on the sampled individuals. Thus a primary incentive of the design methodology was to minimize the cost of achieving a certain "quality" of empirical results, given the differential costs of design points. In this case, quality refers to empirical accuracy of certain parameter estimates. The design point is one of the possible combinations for the values of all the

6. Little attention has been given to experimental design problems in econometrics. Economists have not had, with most conventional research efforts, the ability to control what their data will be. Recently, work with large-scale social experiments has generated interest in this area. See Conlisk and Watts [4], and Conlisk [2, 3].

independent factors. For these problems each observation necessitated giving some payment to an individual or household and, aside from the administrative costs of recording the relevant information on the individual or household's characteristics and behavior patterns, each observation's cost was clearly related to the size of the payment.

On the other hand, the survey research strategy employed in this analysis consisted of mailed questionnaires soliciting each individual's reactions to a set of hypothetical wilderness experiences (see Appendix A). Thus the unit costs of each design point—that is, each hypothetical wilderness experience—were equal. There was, however, another problem that was important for the mail survey: as the number of solicited reactions to hypothetical experiences increased, the length of the questionnaire increased. The sample consisted of a fixed number of individuals who utilized the Spanish Peaks Primitive Area in the summer of 1970, and it was necessary to cover the range of feasible experiences, maintain a reasonable response rate, and test our hypotheses with the most powerful tools and data base available.

A full specification of all the possible wilderness experiences that might legitimately be asked of each sampled individual indicated that 120 to 200 questions would need to be asked of each person when conventional survey research methodology was used. Experience with these surveys suggested that requesting reactions to thirty hypothetical wilderness experiences greatly exceeded the response capability of all of the pretested individuals.[7] Requesting responses to five or ten hypothetical questions was determined to be feasible; beyond this level both the accuracy of response and the response rate were seriously affected. So if the questionnaire were to be kept within a manageable length, every possibility could not be asked of every respondent. Rather, a small subset of the total possible experiences was solicited from any given individual. Our concern was with a reduction in the request for responses to questions regarding experiences asked of each individual, while maintaining the "accuracy" of our estimates.

Thus the primary question that had to be answered in the design of this survey consisted of the selection of a set of recreational experiences that would allow the estimation of our willingness-to-pay

7. These conclusions are based on the survey research experience of Robert Lucas and George Stankey.

functions. Assume that these functions may be rewritten as in Equation (3–5), partitioning the regressors (X) into those variables under the control of the researcher (P) and those that characterize the respondents and are therefore beyond control (Z).

$$y = P\beta_1 + Z\beta_2 + U \qquad\qquad (3\text{–}5)$$

where:

$P = TXK - L$ matrix of observation for each of $K - L$ factors under the control of the researcher (i.e., characteristics of the hypothetical wilderness experiences)

$Z = TXL$ matrix of observation for those regressors, L in number, which are not subject to control (e.g., age, education, etc.)

$\beta_1 = K-LX1$ vector of parameters

$\beta_2 = LX1$ vector of parameters

It is possible to write the OLS estimator for the model in its partitioned form as:

$$\begin{bmatrix} \hat{\beta}_1 \\ \\ \hat{\beta}_2 \end{bmatrix}_{OLS} = \begin{bmatrix} P^TP & P^TZ \\ \\ Z^TP & Z^TZ \end{bmatrix}^{-1} \begin{bmatrix} P^Ty \\ \\ Z^Ty \end{bmatrix} \qquad (3\text{–}6)$$

The variance covariance matrix of these estimated coefficients is given in (3–7).

$$\Sigma_{\hat{\beta}} = \sigma^2 \begin{bmatrix} P^TP & P^TZ \\ Z^TP & Z^TZ \end{bmatrix}^{-1} \qquad (3\text{–}7)$$

It is reasonable to suggest that the characteristics of the hypothetical experiences can be structured to be independent of those describing the respondents. If this independence between the two sets of regressors is upheld, Equation (3–7) can be simplified so that

Equations (3–8a) and (3–8b) describe the variance-covariance matrix for the OLS estimates of β_1 and β_2 respectively.

$$\Sigma_{\hat{\beta}_1} = \sigma^2 (P^T P)^{-1} \tag{3–8a}$$

$$\Sigma_{\hat{\beta}_2} = \sigma^2 (Z^T Z)^{-1} \tag{3–8b}$$

With these equations it is possible to describe formally the objective of the survey effort. It is simply to estimate the effects of the characteristics of a wilderness recreation experience on an individual's willingness-to-pay for such recreation experiences. The pragmatic goal is to measure β_1 as best we can. In terms of Equation (3–8a) the objective is to minimize the diagonal elements of the OLS estimates of β_1's covariance matrix.

Assuming that there are t admissible values for the set of combinations of characteristics that define a wilderness experience, with a_i the ith of them, then $P^T P$ can be rewritten as:

$$P^T P = \sum_{i=1}^{t} n_i a_i^T a_i \tag{3–9}$$

where:

$a_i = 1XK - L$ vector

$n_i =$ the number of times combination a_i is asked ($\sum_{i=1}^{t} n_i =$ sample size)

The problem of experimental design can be expressed as one of selecting the n_i's so as to minimize the diagonal elements of

$$\left(\sum_{i=1}^{t} n_i a_i^T a_i \right)^{-1}$$

If it is assumed that all factors enter linearly so that the willingness-to-pay function is approximated by a first-order polynomial, then there are three conditions that must be satisfied for an orthogonal design to be optimal. Conlisk and Watts [3] outline these assumptions as follows: (1) each design point (that is, each a_i) must cost the same amount; (2) the definition of the range for each factor in the design point vector must be determined by setting upper bounds on the mean squares of these factors; and (3) the objective function must call for minimization of the variance of all the elements of $\hat{\beta}_1$.[8]

An orthogonal design selects sample points so that all factors are independent and the "spread" in the design points is greatest. It would seem that the present problem has many of the characteristics of the orthogonal case. The unit costs are equal for each design point and the objective is to estimate β_1 as accurately as possible. However, there are two important differences. First, one cannot unambiguously select a model with only first-order effects of the design factors. This specification of the model will bias the coefficient estimates if there are higher-order terms in the true model. Thus the choice of a design can be viewed as a tradeoff between variance and bias in the estimation of the response surface.

A second problem associated with the assumptions necessary for an orthogonal design concerns the range of values for the design factors. On the basis of Stankey's [13] research, the control variables chosen for survey utilized in this analysis were: the length of the wilderness trip; the average number of trail encounters per day in the wilderness; and the number of nights in which there was at least one camp encounter. The range for the number of trail encounters was selected to be from zero to three. For the nights of camp encounters it was zero to four, and the length of stay ranged from one to five days.

It should be noted that consistency in the construction of these hypothetical wilderness experiences requires that the nights of camp encounters be bounded by the value implied by the length of trip. Therefore, the feasible region for these variables is restricted. In terms of Figure 3.2 the set of permissible values is similar to *ABCD* and not *OGBCDA*. This consistency check reduces the total number of design points from one hundred to sixty. Thus the second assumption noted by Conlisk and Watts will not be satisfied. Consequently a design was selected that will have maximum flexibility in estimating first- and higher-order response surfaces. It requires an equal number of observations for each design point, with the design points assigned randomly with equal probability to each individual in the sample.

In practice, each respondent was asked to answer five independent

8. See Conlisk and Watts [4], pp. 152–53.

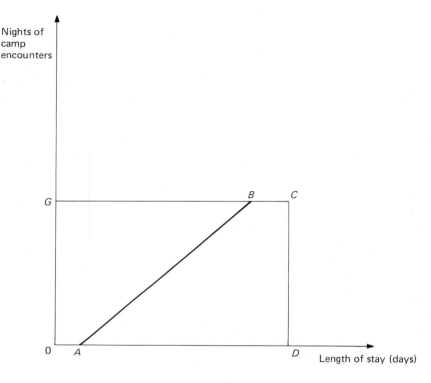

Figure 3-2. Experimental Design Factor Space.

possiblities. Responses to several hypothetical experiences were solicited from each individual for several reasons. These independent answers provided a means of screening the respondents to determine whether they understood the questions and comprehended the differences in the experiences. Additionally, it is reasonable to suspect that the error terms, u_i, will not have constant variance for all individuals within the survey. Thus, the assumption in Equation (3–3b) will not be satisfied. If information on the relative magnitude of variances in the error terms across individuals are available, the objective function can be structured to reflect it as:

$$\theta = (\sum_{i=1}^{t} \sum_{j=1}^{K} v_j b_{ij}^T b_{ij})^{-1} \qquad (3\text{–}10)$$

where

$K =$ number of individual respondents times five

$b_{ij} =$ design point a_i if individual j was asked this experience, zero otherwise.

$\sigma_j^2 = \sigma^2/v_j$ (It should be noted that for some j's, v_j will be constant, because these design points were asked of the same individual)

Since there is no means of determining the v_j's in advance, the design cannot reflect their relative magnitudes. It was possible, however, to estimate their magnitude after the survey had been completed.

The reason for doing this is straightforward. The OLS estimates of the willing-to-pay functions will not be efficient. A more efficient technique would take into account the differences in the variances of the errors across individuals. The five observations per respondent allow the construction of a generalized least-squares estimator, (hereafter GLS) as in Equation (3–11), which is based on the estimates of these variances. This is one of the approaches utilized in the empirical analysis discussed in Chapter 4.

$$\begin{bmatrix} \hat{\beta}_1 \\ \\ \hat{\beta}_2 \end{bmatrix}_{\text{GLS}} = (X^T \hat{\Omega}^{-1} X)^{-1} X^T \hat{\Omega}^{-1} y \tag{3–11}$$

where:

$X = [P \, Z]$
$\hat{\Omega} =$ estimated variance-covariance matrix

THE NATURE OF THE SAMPLE INFORMATION

Approximately six hundred questionnaires were mailed to a sample of wilderness users of the Spanish Peaks Primitive Area in Montana. The sample was compiled by Robert Lucas and George Stankey of the Intermountain Forest and Range Experiment Station. It was designed to be representative of the users of this area during the summer of 1970. Appendix A provides the questionnaire as well as the letters and explanations accompanying the mailings.

Over 40 percent of the questionnaires were returned from the two mailings. A number of these were omitted from the sample because the individual respondents did not or could not answer the questions. These respondents numbered approximately one-third of those returning their questionnaires. Many indicated that they were incapable of quantifying their value for wilderness recreation. Others did not answer and did not indicate reasons. For the most part all respondents indicated the economic and demographic characteristics solicited in the questionnaires.

To investigate whether or not there is a common set of economic and demographic characteristics for the set of individuals who were able to quantify their willingness to pay for hypothetical experiences, a linear probability function was estimated. The dependent variable was dichotomous, with those respondents unable to quantify their willingness to pay assigned a zero and those who could given a one. (Equation (3–12) reports the estimated (with OLS) relationship.

$$\text{Prob of Quantifying} = \underset{(3.426)}{0.574} + \underset{(1.201)}{0.013 EDS} - \underset{(-1.881)}{0.004 AG} \qquad (3\text{–}12)$$

$$\underset{(-0.569)}{-0.002 FY} + \underset{(1.989)}{0.017 WV} + \underset{(1.127)}{0.067 SX}$$

$$\bar{R}^2 = 0.021$$

where

EDS = years of schooling

AG = age in years

FY = income in thousands of dollars

WV = weeks of paid vacation

SX = sex (1 = male, 0 = female)

The numbers in parentheses are t-ratios, testing the null hypothesis of no association. While none of these characteristics appears to be a strong causal factor, age and weeks of paid vacation seem to influence the probability of response. The low $\bar{R}^2$ (coefficient of determination adjusted for degrees of freedom) cannot be interpreted in the usual fashion. It does not have a maximum value of one for these models.[9] Thus it is not possible to provide a general characterization of the socioeconomic characteristics of the actual respondents. The final data base was composed of one hundred and ninety-five individuals, each with five responses to hypothetical wilderness experiences.

SUMMARY AND CONCLUSIONS

This chapter has examined the importance of experimental design for the survey research methodology and the role of econometric estimators for both the design of our survey questionnaires and the estimation of willingness-to-pay functions.

1. Two general specifications will be examined in the empirical research. Economic theory does not provide explicit guidelines for the specification of willingness-to-pay relationships. However, past survey research has provided some evidence that encounters have diminishing marginal effect. A semilog specification has therefore been selected. Additionally, linear forms of the relationship will be estimated.

2. Usually, applied econometric analyses do not have the ability to designate the content of their data base. Rather, they must rely upon existing information gathered for independent administrative purposes. Since the problem requires the solicitation of wilderness users' responses (in terms of their willingness-to-pay) for hypothetical wilderness experiences, the sample survey technique can make use of the powerful results of the experimental design literature.

3. Since the objective is to estimate the effect of each characteristic associated with congestion, an experimental design was selected that provided great flexibility in selecting the order of the response surface and in lowering the variances of the estimated coefficients. The survey technique used is consistent with the

9. See Smith and Cicchetti [11] and Smith [10] for a discussion of OLS estimation of these models, the small sample properties of R^2, and the power of Student t-tests.

reasoning underlying this design. However, it also takes full account of the need for the control variables such as length of trip and nights of camp encounters to be internally consistent.

4. The data source is a cross-section across individuals. It was not expected that the assumption of constant error-term variance, homoscedasticity, would be upheld across individuals. Consequently, an Aitken generalized least-squares estimator was designed to account for these differences in "informational content" or error variance in observations across individuals.

5. Over 40 percent of the six hundred questionnaires were returned from two mailings. Of the returned questionnaires it was observed that some respondents could not or would not report their willingness-to-pay for hypothetical wilderness experiences. Hence these questionnaires were deleted from the sample. An analysis of the socioeconomic characteristics of the respondents who would not or could not quantify their willingness to pay indicates that age and weeks of paid vacation have a small effect upon the probability of quantifying willingness-to-pay. Any associated biases with this last condition will be ignored in the remaining analysis.

REFERENCES

1. C.J. Cicchetti, A.C. Fisher and V.K. Smith, "Economic Models and Planning Outdoor Recreation," *Operations Research* 21 (July/August 1973).

2. J. Conlisk, "When Collinearity is Desirable," *Western Economic Journal* 9 (December 1971).

3. ——, "Experimental Design in Econometrics: The Simultaneous Equations Problem," presented to 1970 annual meetings of the Econometric Society, Detroit.

4. ——, and H. Watts, "A Model for Optimizing Experimental Designs for Estimating Response Surfaces," *Proceedings*, Social Statistic Section, American Statistical Association, 1969.

5. A.S. Goldberger *Econometric Theory* (New York: John Wiley & Sons, 1964).

6. J. Johnston, *Econometric Methods*, 2nd ed. (New York: McGraw-Hill, 1972).

7. R. Lucas, "Wilderness Perception and Use: The Example of the Boundary Waters Canoe Area," *Natural Resources Journal* 3 (July 1964).

8. T.H. Naylor, "Experimental Economics Revisited," *Journal of Political Economy* 80 (March/April 1972).

9. ——, (ed.) *The Design of Computer Simulation Experiments* (Durham, N.C.: Duke University Press, 1969).

10. V.K. Smith, *Monte Carlo Methods: Their Role for Econometrics* (Lexington, Mass.: Lexington Books, D.C. Heath, 1973).

11. ____ and C.J. Cicchetti, "Regression Analysis with Dichotomous Dependent Variables," presented to 1972 Annual Meetings of Econometric Society, Toronto.

12. G.H. Stankey, *The Perception of Wilderness Recreation Carrying Capacity: A Geographic Study in Natural Resource Management*, Ph.D. dissertation, Department of Geography, Michigan State University, 1971.

13. ____, "A Strategy for the Definition and Management of Wilderness Quality," in *Natural Environments: Studies in Theoretical and Applied Analysis*, ed. J.V. Krutilla (Baltimore: Johns Hopkins University Press, 1972).

14. H. Theil, *Principles of Econometrics* (New York: John Wiley & Sons, 1971).

15. K.D. Tocher, "A Note on the Design Problem," *Biometrika* 39 (1952).

16. M.R. Wickens, "A Note on the Use of Proxy Variables," *Econometrica* 40 (July 1972).

Chapter Four

Empirical Results and Their Interpretation

The empirical estimates of the individual willingness-to-pay functions based upon the sample of wilderness users of the Spanish Peaks Primitive Area will be presented in this chapter. Both ordinary least-squares and generalized least-squares estimates of linear and semilog specifications are presented and evaluated.

The first section describes the general nature of the data and the information available for potential inclusion in the willingness-to-pay relationships. In addition, the shortcomings of simple correlation analysis are discussed. The second section presents a sample of the estimated willingness-to-pay equations using both the linear and the semilog forms. A process of sequential estimation was developed to determine "final" equations, and these were then re-estimated with an Aitken generalized least-squares estimator. The specific technique is described in the third section, where the resulting estimates are also presented. The last section summarizes the chapter's conclusions. Appendix B at the back of the book presents an analytical treatment of the relationship between R^2 calculated with ordinary least-squares residuals versus that derived from generalized least-squares residuals.

DESCRIPTION OF THE VARIABLES

The primary variables used in this analysis are defined in Table 4.1. By differentiating the willingness-to-pay measures according to the mode of travel of the party encountered, and not the travel mode of the respondent, it implicitly assumes that this latter factor was not an important determinant of revealed willingness-to-pay. This

Table 4-1. Definition of Variables.

Variable	Description
WBP	Individual willingness to pay per trip when the encounters are with backpacker (hiker) parties, measured in dollars.
WHP	Individual willingness to pay per trip when the encounters are with horseback parties, measured in dollars.
LN	Length of stay of the trip in days.
TN	Number of encounters on the trail per day.
CN	Number of nights of camp encounters.
FY	Income of the household in thousands of dollars.
WV	Weeks of paid vacation of the individual.
SX	Sex of the individual, dichotomous variable (e.g., 1 = male, 0 = female).
ED	Education of the individual in years of schooling.
AG	Age of the individual in years.

assumption is also an empirical question. However, given the limited size of the sample and the additional considerations in the experimental design outlined in Chapter 3, it was not possible to determine the extent to which this assumption holds in practice. The adjustments for heteroscedasticity will reflect some of the effects of the failure of this assumption to hold true by weighting each observation according to the "informational content" or the estimated overall variation in the error associated with each respondent's responses.

Table 4.1 also includes measures of the hypothetical trips and information on the socioeconomic characteristics of the respondent.[1] It should be noted that travel costs were not included in the analysis, even though they were solicited on the questionnaire, because these costs relate to the trip the respondents were engaged in when an initial survey of their preferences was taken, not to the hypothetical trips. However, this travel-cost information was utilized as a benchmark of comparison with the respondent's revealed willingness-to-pay.

1. It should be noted that there does not presently exist a theory of household behavior and its effects on individual consumption decisions. Rather, households are assumed to behave as rational individuals. Robert Michael's [6] recent work on education's effect on nonmarket behavior is a good example. In the original sample of wilderness users, which formed the basis of our mailings, there were several questionnaires solicited from members of a single family. In our survey we selected only one individual from each household.

Table 4-2. Simple Correlation Matrix

	LN	TN	CN	WBP	WHP	EDS	FY	WV	SX	LN²	TN²	CN²
TN	.01											
CN	.50	.00										
WBP	.14	−.05	.00									
WHP	.10	−.06	−.01	.94								
EDS	.02	.02	.00	.10	.07							
FY	−.02	.08	.01	.05	.02	.15						
WV	−.03	−.03	−.05	.13	.13	.13	.05					
SX	−.05	.05	−.06	.11	.10	.19	−.01	.13				
LN²	.98	.01	.49	.14	.11	.02	.08	−.04	−.04			
TN²	.01	.96	.01	−.04	−.05	.03	−.01	−.03	.06	.01		
CN²	.46	.00	.94	.01	.00	.02	.03	−.05	.05	.47	.01	
FY²	−.03	.07	.01	.06	.03	.16	.97	.04	.01	−.02	.07	.03

One might suspect that if the respondent is the household head, the income and education variables would be highly correlated and serve as proxies to some extent. Table 4.2 reports the simple correlation matrix for the variables, and it is clear that the correlations between variables are quite small. It is interesting to note that the relationships between the measures of willingness-to-pay and the encounter variables appear, on the basis of these simple correlations, to be weak.

The apparent independence of these variables stems from two sources. First, the variation in the level of willingness-to-pay is quite large across the sample.[2] Second, there are a number of other factors that determine the willingness-to-pay for a hypothetical wilderness experience, and they cannot be taken into account with simple correlation analysis. Thus there is some incentive to explore the measured effect of the encounter variables when these other factors are simultaneously taken into account.

It is a fairly straightforward process to illustrate the problems caused by failing to take account of these other determinants of willingness-to-pay. Suppose that willingness-to-pay for a trip when the encounters are with hikers is a function of three factors: X_1, X_2, and X_3:

$$WBP = f(X_1, X_2, X_3) \qquad (4\text{–}1)$$

The total change in WBP—$d(WBP)$—can be the result of any or all of these factors, as given in Equation (4–2):

$$d(WBP) = \frac{\partial f}{\partial X_1} \cdot dX_1 + \frac{\partial f}{\partial X_2} \cdot dX_2 + \frac{\partial f}{\partial X_3} \cdot dX_3 \qquad (4\text{–}2)$$

Thus the total change in WBP with a change in, say, X_1, is given as:

$$\frac{d(WBP)}{dX_1} = \frac{\partial f}{\partial X_1} + \frac{\partial f}{\partial X_2} \cdot \frac{dX_2}{dX_1} + \frac{\partial f}{\partial X_3} \cdot \frac{dX_3}{dX_1} \qquad (4\text{–}3)$$

Paralleling Equation (4–3) is a relationship between the simple regression coefficient for WBP and X_1 and the partial regression

2. The specific sample variances for the willingness-to-pay variables are given as follows:

Variance of WBP = 1163.4
Variance of WHP = 1159.0

coefficients.[3] It is possible to show that, if X_1 is related to X_2 and/or X_3, there may be a strong partial effect—i.e., in terms of $\partial f / \partial X_1$ in Equation 4–3—with little or no perceived total effect. The reason for this is that there may be offsetting effects resulting from X_2 and X_3. Moreover, the simple regression coefficient and simple correlation coefficient are easily related as suggested by:

$$b = \frac{{}^s WBP}{s_{X_1}} \cdot {}^r WBP, X_1 \tag{4-4}$$

where

b = simple regression coefficient for $WBP = f(X_1)$

${}^s WBP$ = standard deviation for WBP

${}^s X_1$ = standard deviation for X_1

${}^r WBP, X_1$ = simple correlation coefficient between WBP and X_1

Equation (4–4) indicates that, *certeris paribus*, either the offsetting effects of other variables or a large degree of variation in WBP can make the simple correaltion between two variables quite small.

In what follows, alternative functional forms and specifications are outlined and examined in order to infer the relationship between willingness-to-pay and encounters. The estimated equations have been selected for inclusion in order to give some notion of the testing process performed, but without presenting a great deal of irrelevant intermediate material. In addition to the alternative functional forms, variables were entered in different fashions—most notable age, using interval dummy variables.[4] Since none of these specifications appeared superior to those presented, details of these regression estimates are not included.

ORDINARY LEAST-SQUARES ESTIMATES: LINEAR AND SEMILOG WILLINGNESS-TO-PAY FUNCTIONS

As noted in Chapter 3, linear and semilog specifications of the willingness-to-pay functions were considered. Each implies a

3. See Goldberger [3], pp. 27–38.
4. This procedure attempts to account for nonlinearities in a fashion similar to spline functions. See Poirier [7].

different effect for the encounter variables on individual willingness-to-pay. Tables 4.3 and 4.4 present a sample of the linear specifications that were considered in the course of this analysis. The first of these relates to the effects of encounters with backpacking parties, while the second deals with encounters with horseback riders.

It should be noted that linear and quadratic forms of the encounter and length-of-trip variables were examined. Recall that the survey design allowed this flexibility—that is, in order to avoid

Table 4-3. Linear Willingness-to-Pay Functions for Encounters with Backing Parties (OLS)[a]

	Equations					
Variable	(1)	(2)	(3)	(4)	(5)	(6)
LN	5.646	5.130	4.511	4.303	5.016	5.163
	(1.167)	(5.297)	(0.980)	(0.933)	(5.180)	(5.309)
LN^2	- .079	—	.091	.131	—	—
	(- 0.109)		(0.133)	(0.190)		
TN	- 2.297	- 2.299	-1.809	-1.797	- 1.862	-1.804
	(- 0.676)	(- 0.677)	(-1.864)	(-1.849)	(- 1.925)	(-1.856)
TN^2	.161	.162	—	—	—	—
	(0.151)	(0.152)				
CN	- 4.136	- 4.043	-2.342	-2.338	- 2.283	-2.350
	(- 1.492)	(- 1.534)	(-2.321)	(-2.313)	(- 2.272)	(-2.326)
CN^2	.521	.495	—	—	—	—
	(0.685)	(1.304)				
FY	- 1.290	- 1.290	.211	.262	.106	.256
	(- 1.977)	(- 1.977)	(1.251)	(1.567)	(0.635)	(1.575)
FY^2	.043	.043	—	—	—	—
	(2.239)	(2.240)				
SX	5.615	5.611	6.423	7.321	5.867	7.287
	(2.360)	(2.360)	(2.721)	(3.122)	(2.469)	(3.110)
ED	.582	.581	.895	—	.672	—
	(1.305)	(1.304)	(2.036)		(1.507)	
AG	.263	.263	—	—	.250	—
	(3.028)	(3.029)			(2.875)	
WV	1.055	1.056	1.018	1.078	1.020	1.073
	(3.642)	(3.647)	(3.502)	(3.723)	(3.522)	(3.708)
Int.	-10.866	-10.171	.501	-5.598	-20.930	-6.609
	(- 0.994)	(- 1.145)	(0.051)	(-0.714)	(- 2.844)	(-1.435)
$\bar{R}^2$	.064	.065	.040	.051	.062	.052
F	6.50	7.10	6.03	8.48	9.04	9.90

[a]The numbers in parentheses are Student' t-rations for the null hypothesis. H_0: α_i = 0. $\bar{R}^2$ is the coefficient of determination adjusted for degrees of freedom. F is the F-statistic for the test of the overall relationship.

Table 4-4. Linear Willingness-to-Pay Functions for Encounters with Horseriding Parties (OLS)[a]

	Equations					
	(1)	*(2)*	*(3)*	*(4)*	*(5)*	*(6)*
LN	−1.624	3.959	−2.301	−2.414	3.853	3.968
	(−0.333)	(4.055)	(−0.500)	(−0.521)	(3.950)	(4.060)
LN^2	.848	—	.950	.972	—	—
	(1.169)		(1.378)	(1.410)		
TN	−4.347	−4.326	−2.045	−2.039	− 2.078	−2.027
	(−1.270)	(−1.264)	(−2.096)	(−2.089)	(− 2.133)	(−2.075)
TN^2	.751	.748	—	—	—	—
	(0.698)	(0.097)				
CN	−3.172	−4.179	−2.098	−2.095	− 2.074	−2.135
	(−1.135)	(−1.573)	(−2.067)	(−2.065)	(− 2.049)	(−2.103)
CN^2	.306	.595	—	—	—	—
	(0.389)	(0.819)				
FY	−1.012	−1.018	.105	.132	.022	.138
	(−1.540)	(−1.548)	(0.616)	(0.787)	(0.131)	(0.844)
FY^2	.032	.032	—	—	—	—
	(1.631)	(1.640)				
SX	5.320	5.366	6.091	6.553	5.609	6.615
	(2.219)	(2.239)	(2.546)	(2.782)	(2.343)	(2.809)
ED	.213	.221	.486	—	.303	—
	(0.473)	(0.493)	(1.101)		(0.674)	
AG	.235	.236	—	—	.228	—
	(2.678)	(2.692)			(2.612)	
WV	1.078	1.072	1.045	1.078	1.040	1.069
	(3.692)	(3.671)	(3.576)	(3.707)	(3.566)	(3.673)
Int.	5.950	−1.558	.501	7.030	−10.915	−1.829
	(0.540)	(−0.174)	(0.051)	(0.892)	(− 1.472)	(−0.395)
$\bar{R}^2$	.046	.045	.040	.040	.045	.039
F	4.89	5.20	6.03	6.72	6.67	7.50

[a]The numbers in parentheses are Student *t*-ratios for the null hypotheses. $H_0: \alpha_i = 0. \bar{R}^2$ is the coefficient of determination adjusted for degrees of freedom. *F* is the *F*-statistic for the test of the overall relationship.

estimation bias, a design was selected that was consistent with a large number of models. The first equation in each table presents the relationship with all variables entered. Through a simple sequential process, alternative combinations of omitted variables have been examined, and equations (2) through (5) in each table are a sample of these.

The decision rule which was applied to each specification was to determine whether or not particular variables should be retained or omitted from the relationship was based on: (a) the conformity of the sign of the estimated coefficient with that expected, *a priori;* and (b) the estimated student *t*-statistic for the null hypothesis of no association. Until recently little attention has been given by econometricians to the properties of their "data mining" or sequential selection rules for estimating economic models. Research in this area is still in the early stages.[5] The properties of sequential estimators such as the one utilized in this study are not well understood. However, some generalizations are possible for the most simple cases.

For the two-regressor case, Wallace and Ashar [10] have shown that the relationship between the size of the ratio of the square of the true value of the coefficient for the variable being considered for inclusion, to the variance in the OLS estimate of it, and a pre-defined constant allows one to discriminate between the OLS estimator and the sequential techinque in terms of their respective mean squared errors. Without knowledge of the ratio *a priori*, the best we can hope for is improvement in the sequential estimator in terms of mean squared error through adjustments to the level of significance of the test of the null hypothesis of no association. However, without further information on the form of the model, or prior expectations on the magnitude of certain variables, true coefficients, it is difficult to discriminate between these alternative sequential approaches. The technique selected here has the advantage of being powerful in detecting cases where the true value of the coefficient is zero.

A review of the estimated coefficients in Tables 4.3 and 4.4 indicates that the coefficients for most of the variables in the final equations (designated number (6) in each table) are reasonably stable over the alternative specifications considered.

The selection of an approach for sequential estimation is further complicated by the fact that most, if not all, of the analysis of alternative techniques has focused on the mean squared error of the estimates. This specification of the objective function for estimator selection gives equal weight to the variance and squared bias of the estimates. For many applications the appropriate weighting may be unequal.

Accordingly, in the absence of further information on the properties of the alternative decision rules, and because the estimated

---

5. For a more detailed review of the alternative sequential techniques and their properties, see Smith and Bich [8].

coefficients for the variables of principle interest are quite stable, a sequential technique was selected. It is based on agreement between the *a priori* sign with that of the estimated coefficient and a pretest with the student *t*-statistic. As Wallace and Ashar [10 pp. 184-85] have noted

> There are costs to ignorance that cannot be avoided by statistical procedures. If we are not sure *a priori* whether a particular variable(s) belongs in a model, pretesting . . . will, on average, yield estimators that are sure to be worse than least squares estimators derived from an accurate prior specification. And the other side of the coin is that data can tell us something valuable about specifications.

In some cases the choice of a "best" equation amounted to a decision on which proxy variables were preferred. For example, in Table 4.3, equation (5), the education and age variables are, presumably, correlated with the income variable, thus making it difficult to distinguish and individual effect for income. In equation (6), with these variables omitted, the coefficient for income is significantly different from zero using a one-tailed test at the 90 percent level.

For the final equations with the linear specification (i.e., equations (6) in Tables 4.3 and 4.4), all variables have the anticipated signs, and, with the exception of income, are significantly different from zero at the 95 percent level of accuracy. It would appear from these estimates that camp encounters have a greater deleterious effect upon individual willingness-to-pay for wilderness recreation at the Spanish Peaks than do trail encounters. However, statistical testing of this proposition (i.e., $H_0: a_{CN} - a_{TN} = 0$) failed to reject the null hypothesis.

Tables 4.5 and 4.6 report the estimated willingness-to-pay functions using the semilog specification for encounters with hikers and horseback riders. Once again a sample has been included from the trial equations, which indicates the pretesting and sequential process utilized to derive final equations. In this case the final specifications are numbered as equation (7) in each table. The variables that enter these final equations are essentially the same as with the linear form. The length of trip variable (*LN*) admits a quadratic effect upon the logarithm of willingness-to-pay. Income (*FY*) does not enter the equation estimated for willingness-to-pay

Table 4-5. Semilog Willingness-to-Pay for Encounters with Backpacking Parties (OLS)[a]

Variable	Equations						
	(1)	(2)	(3)	(4)	(5)	(6)	(7)
LN	0.889 (3.519)	0.954 (3.983)	0.890 (3.522)	0.279 (5.497)	0.935 (3.886)	0.945 (3.952)	0.934 (3.887)
LN^2	-.092 (-2.466)	-.102 (-2.872)	-.093 (-2.464)	—	-.099 (-2.765)	-.101 (-2.848)	-.099 (-2.763)
TN	.026 (0.145)	.025 (0.142)	-.114 (-2.247)	.024 (0.132)	-.114 (-2.255)	-.111 (-2.211)	-.114 (-2.249)
TN^2	-.046 (-0.818)	-.045 (-0.815)	—	-.045 (-0.810)	—	—	—
CN	-.106 (-0.728)	-.211 (-4.021)	-.108 (-0.745)	-.005 (0.034)	-.211 (-4.001)	-.211 (-4.019)	-.211 (-4.011)
CN^2	-.031 (-0.785)	—	-.031 (-0.782)	-.063 (-1.664)	—	—	—
FY	-.014 (-0.400)	-.015 (-0.432)	-.014 (-0.395)	-.013 (-0.382)	.013 (1.420)	—	.013 (1.513)
FY^2	.001 (0.711)	.001 (0.730)	.001 (0.703)	.001 (0.689)	—	—	—
WV	.040 (2.663)	.040 (2.662)	.041 (2.687)	.041 (2.702)	.045 (2.990)	.041 (2.696)	.045 (2.987)
SX	.236 (1.901)	.236 (1.895)	.234 (1.880)	.231 (1.855)	.302 (2.457)	.229 (1.854)	.307 (2.513)
ED	.078 (3.328)	.077 (3.309)	.077 (3.312)	.077 (3.278)	—	.080 (3.560)	—
AG	-.001 (-0.179)	-.001 (-0.163)	-.001 (-0.228)	-.001 (-0.208)	.001 (-0.319)	—	—
Int.	-1.093 (-1.912)	-1.128 (-1.980)	-1.028 (-1.816)	-.271 (-0.582)	-.248 (-0.587)	-1.162 (-2.134)	-.214 (-0.524)
$\bar{R}^2$	.064	.064	.064	.059	.055	.066	.056
F	6.53	7.07	7.07	6.54	8.08	10.81	9.23

[a]The numbers in parentheses are Student t-ratios for the null hypothesis, $H_0 : \alpha_i = 0$. $\bar{R}^2$ is the coefficient of determination adjusted for degrees of freedom. F is the F-statistic for the test of the overall relationship.

Table 4-6. Semilog Willingness-to-Pay for Encounters with Horseriding Parties (OLS)[a]

				Equations			
Variable	*(1)*	*(2)*	*(3)*	*(4)*	*(5)*	*(6)*	*(7)*
LN	0.633 (2.112)	0.665 (2.344)	0.633 (2.114)	0.252 (4.192)	0.664 (2.340)	0.675 (2.380)	0.671 (2.367)
LN^2	-.058 (-1.299)	-.063 (-1.485)	-.058 (-1.299)		-.063 (-1.480)	-.063 (-1.511)	-.063 (-1.500)
TN	-.143 (-0.677)	-.143 (-0.679)	-.201 (-3.361)	-.144 (-0.684)	-.201 (-3.370)	-.207 (-3.473)	-.207 (-3.466)
TN^2	-.019 (-0.290)	-.019 (-0.289)	—	-.019 (-0.289)	—	—	—
CN	-.233 (-1.358)	-.286 (-4.593)	-.234 (-1.365)	-.164 (-1.006)	-.287 (-4.611)	-.288 (-4.637)	-.288 (-4.636)
CN^2	-.016 (-0.331)	—	-.016 (-0.330)	-.035 (-0.791)	—	—	—
FY	-.046 (-1.134)	-.046 (-1.148)	-.046 (-1.132)	-.046 (-1.124)	-.013 (-1.238)	—	—
FY^2	.001 (0.803)	.001 (0.812)	.001 (0.801)	.001 (0.793)	—	—	—
WV	.046 (2.555)	.046 (2.556)	.046 (2.565)	.046 (2.579)	.045 (2.524)	.044 (2.476)	.045 (2.549)
SX	.247 (1.674)	.246 (1.672)	.246 (1.667)	.244 (1.652)	.264 (1.800)	.271 (1.854)	.285 (1.973)
ED	.013 (0.457)	.012 (0.449)	.013 (0.451)	.012 (0.435)	.019 (0.699)	.014 (0.521)	—
AG	.006 (1.082)	.006 (1.089)	.006 (1.067)	.006 (1.066)	—	—	—
Int.	.297 (0.438)	.280 (0.414)	.325 (0.484)	.810 (1.471)	.145 (0.240)	.020 (0.033)	.219 (0.480)
$\bar{R}^2$	.044	.045	.045	.043	.046	.045	.046
F	4.71	5.14	5.14	4.98	6.85	7.61	8.84

[a]The numbers in parentheses are Student t-ratios for the null hypothesis, $H_0 : \alpha_i = 0$. $\bar{R}^2$ is the coefficient of determination adjusted for degrees of freedom. F is the F-statistic for the test of the overall relationship.

when the encounters are with horseback riders, due to an incorrect sign and a large standard error.

For most of the independent variables, the student *t*-ratios for the null hypothesis of no association are somewhat higher using this form than with the linear specification. The coefficients of determination should not be directly compared since the dependent variables are not measured in the same scale in the linear and semilog forms.

Both functional forms appear to perform reasonably well, so that the ultimate choice between them must be made on an *a priori* basis. While it is true that economic theory does not provide an explicit functional form for individual willingness-to-pay schedules, it is possible to derive some tentative guidelines. For example, there is good reason to suspect that encounters will have a diminishing marginal effect—the fifth encounter on the trail during a given time interval is likely to have a smaller effect upon willingness-to-pay than the first, for instance. Since the linear specification implies that each encounter has the same effect upon willingness-to-pay, it cannot capture this kind of behavior. As noted previously, the semilog form presupposes that each encounter has the same percentage impact on willingness-to-pay. Thus, as the total willingness-to-pay declines, the absolute effect of an additional encounter diminishes. Clearly it is a big step between this particular functional form and the behavioral postulate of diminishing marginal effects of encounters. Consequently, both forms have been estimated, and their use will be illustrated with the semilog function. This choice should not be construed to imply that the linear form would not have performed well in these analyses. Rather it reflects a judgment that the semilog specification is a more reasonable functional representation for individual willingness-to-pay.

HETEROSCEDASTICITY AND AITKEN ESTIMATION

Cross-sectional data characteristically exhibit a problem of heteroscedasticity with the disturbances of the linear regression model.[6] That is, the assumption of constant variance (i.e., $E(u_i^2) = \sigma^2$) stated in Chapter 3 is not satisfied. There are any number of

---

6. In this case linear refers to the fact that the model is linear in parameters, not necessarily that it is a linear equation.

reasons that may underlie such nonspherical errors. Since the data used in the analysis represent a survey of wilderness users' responses to hypothetical wilderness experiences, the problem can arise from either the characteristics of the individuals or the nature of the questions. The second possibility can be dismissed fairly readily. Each individual has an equal probability of receiving any particular question, thus there should be no dependence between the first or second or any other question addressed to each of the respondents. Moreover, the specification accounts for those factors that distinguish one experience from another. Thus, the other possibility—namely, the characteristics of the respondents that have not been accounted for—seems to be a potentially important source for differences in the errors' variance.

In Chapter 3 it was observed that the design of the experiment anticipated this possibility by soliciting responses to questions regarding five independent, hypothetical wilderness experiences from each sampled individual. It is possible to use the ordinary least squares (OLS) residuals to determine whether or not heteroscedasticity is a problem, and if it is to construct an estimate of the error-covariance matrix in order to adjust for it.[7]

In Chapter 3 the model described was stated as:

$$y = P\beta_1 + Z\beta_2 + U \tag{4-5}$$

where P is a matrix of factors under the control of the survey researcher and Z a matrix of variables outside the researcher's control, such as the characteristics of the individual respondents. Rearranging the respective matrices Equation (4–5) can be written as:

$$y = [P\,Z] \begin{bmatrix} \beta_1 \\ \beta_2 \end{bmatrix} + U \tag{4-6}$$

or

$$y = X\beta + U \tag{4-7}$$

7. If the estimate of the errors' covariance structure is consistent, then the estimates are consistent. Moreover, the Aitken estimator is asymptotically efficient and asymptotically normal. For additional discussion see Kmenta [5], pp. 499–508.

This simplification makes it possible to describe the OLS residuals, ϵ, as in Equation (4–8):

$$\epsilon = [I - X(X^TX)^{-1}X^T]y \qquad (4–8)$$

This means that even if the true errors are homoscedastic [i.e., $E(u_i^2)$ $= \sigma^2$ for all i], the OLS residuals are not. This can be demonstrated by deriving $E(\epsilon \, \epsilon^T)$, as a first step note:

$$\epsilon \, \epsilon^T = [I - X(X^TX)^{-1}X^T]y \, y^T \, [I - X(X^TX)^{-1}X^T]^T \qquad (4–9)$$

Given the assumptions of the model as stated in equation (3–2), $E[y \, y^T] = \sigma^2 I$ with homoscedastic errors.[8] This simplifies $E[\epsilon \, \epsilon^T]$ as shown by:

$$E[\epsilon \, \epsilon^T] = \sigma^2 [I - X(X^TX)^{-1}X^T] \qquad (4–10)$$

since

$$[I - X(X^TX)^{-1}X^T]^T[I - X(X^TX)^{-1}X^T] = I - X(X^TX)^{-1}X^T.$$

The heteroscedasticity of the OLS residuals suggests that they cannot be used to estimate directly the appropriate covariance matrix. However, they can be used to suggest that each individual's error's variance is proportional to the sum of squared OLS residuals across the five responses, as in (4–11).[9] The rationale for this estimator stems from Kmenta's [5] outline of an iterative approach for computing the maximum likelihood (ML) estimates of the model's parameters, including the covariance structure. We use the first-round estimates of the variances. Thus our parameter estimates will only be asymptotically equivalent to the ML estimates. An alternative approach might call for the use of

$$\sigma_j^2 = \sigma^2 \, [\, \sum_{i=1}^{5} (\epsilon_{ij})^2 \,] \qquad (4–11)$$

8. This proposition can be demonstrated fairly readily in the simple linear regression model. Suppose $y_i = \alpha + \beta X_i + \epsilon_i$ where ϵ_i is the stochastic error with an expected value of zero and a variance of σ^2. Then we have:

$$\mathrm{Var}\,(y_i^2) = E[y_i - E(y_i)]^2 = E[(\alpha + \beta X_i + \epsilon_i) - (\alpha + \beta X_i)]^2 = E(\epsilon_i^2) = \sigma^2$$

The generalization to N observations is straightforward.

9. It should be noted that P varies across the five responses of each individual while X does not.

where

ϵ_{ij} = OLS residual for the ith question posed to the jth respondent. However, it is possible to show, using Khintchine's theorem, that this approach is asymptotically equivalent to that outlined below.

$$\sum_{i} (\hat{\epsilon}_{ij} - \bar{\hat{\epsilon}}_{j})^2 .$$

The variation in these sums of squared OLS residuals is sufficiently great across individuals so as not to be the result of the inherent heteroscedasticity in ϵ_{ij} resulting from variations in the experiences solicited. For example, the ratio of the largest sum of squared residuals for a given individual to the smallest within the sample respondents, using the semilog specification and the willingness-to-pay derived for encounters with hikers, is over six hundred. Thus there are substantial discrepancies in the "informational content" (i.e., underlying error variance) of each respondent's replies. Generalized least-squares estimation will take these differences into account in the estimation process, and thereby yield a more efficient set of estimates. This conclusion is, of course, conditioned by the estimate of the error's covariance matrix. It is not known, *a priori*, what the exact nature of the error's structure is. Rather it is assumed that an estimate of the conditional sum of squared residuals for each individual respondent will provide a reasonably good approximation. Most surveys have but only one observation to determine this covariance structure; in this study there are five, which makes the estimates more credible.

Tables 4.7 and 4.8 provide the Aitken (GLS) estimates for each of the final equations from the preceding tables (i.e., equations (6) in Tables 4.3 and 4.4 and equations (7) in Tables 4.5 and 4.6). It should be noted that there is a different estimated variance-covariance matrix corresponding to each of these equations. For example, the GLS estimates of the linear willingness-to-pay schedule for encounters with backpackers are based on the OLS residuals from its counterpart. In all cases the improvement in the efficiency of estimation is evidenced by the great increase in t-ratios. The estimated standard errors for the coefficient estimates are one-half or less of the values of the OLS estimates.[10] These findings conform to Goldfeld and Quandt's [4] findings with sampling experiments. They

10. See Goldfeld and Quandt [4], pp. 78–123, for a discussion of the alternative approaches for adjusting for heteroscedasticity. Our approach falls within the general class suggested by Kmenta [5], pp. 264–67.

Table 4-7. Generalized Least-Squares Estimates of Willingness-to-Pay Functions: Encounters with Backpacking Parties[a]

Variable	Linear	Semilog
LN	4.141	.780
	(19.249)	(8.750)
LN^2	—	− .069
		(−5.217)
TN	− 1.211	− .083
	(− 5.345)	(−4.601)
CN	− 1.723	− .152
	(− 7.685)	(−8.044)
FY	.140	.020
	(3.432)	(6.189)
WV	1.123	.057
	(14.838)	(8.308)
SX	5.188	.362
	(10.703)	(8.258)
Int.	− 5.048	− .354
	(− 5.388)	(−2.322)
$\overline{R}*^2$	.694	.756

[a] The numbers in parentheses are student t-ratios for the null hypothesis, H_0: $\alpha_i = 0$. $\overline{R}*^2$ is the coefficient of determination adjusted for degrees of freedom.

Table 4-8. Generalized Least-Squares Estimates of Willingness-to-Pay Functions: Encounters with Horse-Riding Parties[a]

Variable	Linear	Semilog
LN	3.167	.672
	(14.678)	(6.798)
LN^2	—	− .056
		(− 3.876)
TN	− 1.123	(− .141)
	(− 5.114)	(− 7.526)
CN	− 1.647	− .205
	(− 7.494)	(−10.096)
FY	.063	—
	(1.902)	
WV	.885	.056
	(9.703)	(8.604)
SX	3.721	.260
	(7.642)	(5.616)
Int.	− 1.829	− .045
	(− 2.037)	(− 0.277)
$\overline{R}*^2$	.516	.721

[a] The numbers in parentheses are Student t-ratios for the null hypothesis, H_0: $\alpha_i = 0$. $\overline{R}*^2$ is the coefficient of determination adjusted for degrees of freedom.

have noted [4, pp. 118-19] that "the results from the sampling experiments suggest that heteroscedasticity can be a quantitatively severe problem."

The coefficients of determination ($\bar{R}^{*2}$) reported in Tables 4.7 and 4.8 are not directly comparable with those of the OLS estimates (i.e., $\bar{R}^2$) since they do not permit the same interpretation as when $\bar{R}^2$ is used with OLS. In the latter case the total sum of squares of the residuals may be partitioned into two components. Such a partitioning is not possible with Aitken residuals.[11] Consequently, an alternative measure of "goodness of fit" is reported. An Aitken estimation may be constructed by transforming the data to reflect the weights that heteroscedasticity requires, then estimating the relationships with OLS and the transformed data. The estimated coefficient of determination under the new definition is $\bar{R}^{*2}$. It is adjusted for degrees of freedom and is based on residuals estimated using the predictions from GLS equations and the transformed dependent variables. In this case the sum of squared residuals will partition orthogonally and $\bar{R}^{*2}$ will be confined to the zero-to-one interval. It should be noted that the heteroscedasticity adjustment does reduce the total variation in the transformed dependent variables. Thus, $\bar{R}^2$ and $\bar{R}^{*2}$ are not comparable statistics.

SUMMARY AND CONCLUSIONS

The equations estimated from the survey data provide strong support for the hypotheses that (1) solitude is an important characteristic of wilderness or low-density recreation, as suggested in Chapters 2 and 3; and (2) encounters reflect the disruptions of solitude resulting from increased intensities of use of a given area and the congestion that results. Accordingly, the equations indicate that the revealed individual willingness-to-pay will exhibit a significant negative relationship with encounter variables. In addition several further remarks may bear repetition.

1. In Chapter 3 it was noted that over 40 percent of the sample responded to the questionnaires. However, a subset of these respondents was unable to express its willingness-to-pay for hypothetical wilderness experiences.

11. For a more detailed discussion of the implications of this problem, see Appendix B.

2. Analysis of the simple correlation coefficients of the data collected in the survey seemed to indicate that encounters and willingness-to-pay for a wilderness experience were not related. However, in assessing the interpretation of these results, it was noted that large variation in the willingness-to-pay variable and/or important additional determinants of willingness-to-pay will tend to confound the results derived from such analyses. Therefore, a multiple-regression approach was used to identify the individual effect of encounters upon willingness-to-pay while accounting for other possible determining factors.

3. Both linear and semilog specifications for the individual willingness-to-pay relationships were estimated with ordinary least squares. A sequential procedure for entering alternative independent variables was used in order to isolate a "final" equation when the encounters were with backpackers and horse riders and when the functions were linear and semilog.

4. There is little basis for selecting between the two functional forms. While it is true that the magnitude of the Student *t*-ratios for the null hypothesis of no association is somewhat greater with the semilog specification, these findings are not sufficient to warrant selection of one on the basis of this statistical criterion alone. However, when the economics of consumer behavior and some limited additional survey research evidence are also considered, it is reasonable to select the semilog specification over the linear form.

5. Since heteroscedasticity is likely to be a serious problem with cross-sectional survey research (and, in fact, the data indicate evidence of fairly great divergences in the estimated error variances across individual respondents), efficient estimation required an Aitken generalized least-squares estimator. The estimated error covariance structure was derived by assuming that the error variances were proportional to the magnitude of the sum of squared OLS residuals for each individual respondent.

6. GLS estimation provided a rather dramatic increase in the efficiency of the estimates and therefore improved the ability to perceive the effects of congestion upon individual willingness-to-pay.

Efforts to measure the effects of congestion upon individual satisfaction seem to have been reasonably successful. Consequently, it is necessary to address the implications of such estimates for both the management of existing low-density recreational facilities and for those allocation decisions involving a choice of development or preservation of a wilderness or similar facility. In Chapters 5 and 6 case studies will be analyzed to illustrate the use of the willingness-to-pay functions just estimated for both the allocation of scarce resources to management and investment decisions.

REFERENCES

1. C.J. Cicchetti, "A Multivariate Statistical Analysis of Wilderness Users," in *Natural Environments: Studies in Theoretical and Applied Analysis*, ed. J.V. Krutilla (Baltimore: Johns Hopkins University Press, 1972).

2. A.S. Goldberger, *Econometric Theory* (New York: John Wiley & Sons, 1964).

3. ———, *Topics in Regression Analysis* (New York: Macmillan, 1968).

4. S.M. Goldfeld and R.E. Quandt, *Nonlinear Methods in Econometrics* (Amsterdam: North Holland, 1972).

5. Jan Kmenta, *Elements of Econometrics* (New York: Macmillan, 1971).

6. Robert T. Michael, "Education in Non Market Production," *Journal of Political Economy* 81 (March/April 1973).

7. D.J. Poirier, "Multiple Regression Using Bilinear Splines," Social Systems Research Institute Paper #7230, University of Wisconsin, October 1972.

8. V. Kerry Smith and T. Bich, "Specification Analysis and Post Data Model Evaluation: A Review," unpublished paper, 1974.

9 George H. Stankey, "A Strategy for the Definition and Management of Wilderness Quality," in *Natural Environments: Studies in Theoretical and Applied Analysis*, ed. J.V. Krutilla (Baltimore: Johns Hopkins University Press, 1972).

10. T.D. Wallace and V.G. Ashar, "Sequential Methods in Model Construction," *Review of Economics and Statistics* 54 (May 1972).

Chapter Five

Applications of the Willingness-to-Pay Relationships

In Chapter 4 a relationship was estimated between an individual's willingness-to-pay for wilderness experiences and a set of variables describing the quantity and quality of those experiences, as well as the characteristics of the specific individual. These empirical results are more illustrative than definitive. They are based on a survey of limited scope and are only relevant for a specific area, the Spanish Peaks Primitive Area.[1] The objective has been to propose and illustrate a general methodology that can be used for estimating the congestion cost associated with crowding. In this chapter two applications that rely on such empirical relationships will be presented. The first will deal with the problem of determining the optimal level of use of a scarce resource. The second will be a dynamic investment-related application.

As noted in Chapter 1, the demand for wilderness recreation has grown rapidly and is beginning to force consideration of the allocation of land among alternative uses. In general, the problem is to allocate resources to their highest valued use. In the case of wildlands there are some rather unique factors associated with the allocation decision. Low-density wilderness recreation requires the services of pristine natural areas. Thus, when a decision between preservation and development must be made it is necessary to take into account the irreversibility of the development alternative.[2] This

---

1. These assumptions mean that the user's preferences and anticipations are identical to those sampled at the Spanish Peaks Area, and the Area's characteristics that are not accounted for in the relationship are not significantly different from those of the Spanish Peaks.
2. For a more detailed discussion see Fisher, Krutilla, and Cicchetti [3].

irreversibility is also present when wilderness areas are utilized for higher-density recreational activities. Consequently, in evaluating these allocation decisions it is necessary to measure the effects of increased levels of use on the quality of the wilderness recreation derived from existing areas and from any potential new allocations. For the dynamic analysis a generalization of the Krutilla-Cicchetti [4] methodology will be undertaken. However, the fact that this application is based upon data for the Spanish Peaks must be noted. Any inferences drawn for other resources require the assumptions that both the area's and user's characteristics are similar to the sample utilized in this analysis. It is worth repeating that the purpose of these applications is to develop a methodology rather than to develop parameters that policymakers may readily put into any evaluation functions.

The basic premise underlying both examples is that in the case of low-density wilderness recreation, an increase in the levels of use for a fixed set of wilderness areas is not necessarily synonymous with an increase in the benefit stream to be derived from these facilities. That is, there may be congestion costs associated with crowding that reduce the satisfaction an individual derives from such experiences. Before addressing the specific problems, the first of the models discussed in Chapter 2 will be reviewed to illustrate the effects of congestion on Pareto-efficient choices.

Consider a two-commodity world in which each individual can select either X_1 (representing a composite market good) or W (representing the wilderness recreational services). The total use level of a given set of areas capable of providing low-density recreation is assumed to affect individual utility, therefore equation (5–1) can be used to represent the ith individual's utility function.

$$U_i = U^i (X_{1i}, W_i, W) \qquad\qquad (5\text{–}1)$$

where

U_i = utility of the ith individual

X_{1i} = ith individual's consumption of X_1

W_i = ith individual's consumption of W

$W = \sum_i W_i$

To derive the Pareto-efficient conditions, maximize the utility of one individual subject to the constraint that the use of others remains at a constant utility level. If it is assumed that there are T total resources available for consumption and that the cost functions of X_1 and W are separable, one can write the Paretian objective function as:

$$G = U^m(X_{1m}, W_m, W) \qquad (5\text{-}2)$$

$$+ \sum_{i=1}^{m-1} \lambda_i[U^i(X_{1i}, W_i, W) - s_i] +$$

$$+ \mu[\sum_{i=1}^{m} X_{1i} - X_1] + \phi[\sum_{i=1}^{m} W_i - W] +$$

$$+ \theta[T - C_1(X_1) - C_w(W)]$$

where:

λ_i, μ, ϕ, and θ are Lagrangian multipliers

$C_1(\ )$ and $C_w(\ )$ are cost functions for X_1 and W, respectively

s_i is the level of utility to which the ith individual is held

Maximizing G, the following first-order conditions result:

$$\frac{\partial G}{\partial X_{1i}} = \lambda_i\left(\frac{\partial U^i}{\partial X_{1i}}\right) + \mu = 0 \qquad i = 1, \ldots, (m-1) \qquad (5\text{-}3)$$

$$\frac{\partial G}{\partial W_i} = \lambda_i\left(\frac{\partial U^i}{\partial W_i}\right) + \phi = 0 \qquad i = 1, \ldots, (m-1) \qquad (5\text{-}4)$$

$$\frac{\partial G}{\partial X_1} = -\mu - \left[\theta\left(\frac{\partial C_1}{\partial X_1}\right)\right] = 0 \qquad (5\text{-}5)$$

$$\frac{\partial G}{\partial W} = \sum_{i=1}^{m-1} \lambda\left(\frac{\partial U^i}{\partial W}\right) + \left(\frac{\partial U^m}{\partial W}\right) - \phi - \theta\left(\frac{\partial C_w}{\partial W}\right) = 0 \qquad (5\text{-}6)$$

$$\frac{\partial G}{\partial X_{1m}} = \left(\frac{\partial U^m}{\partial X_{1m}}\right) + \mu = 0 \qquad (5\text{-}7)$$

$$\frac{\partial G}{\partial W_m} = \frac{\partial U^m}{\partial W_m} + \phi = 0 \qquad (5\text{-}8)$$

as well as the partial derivatives with respect to λ_i, μ, ϕ, and θ.

Simply stated, these conditions imply that the marginal rate of substitution in consumption between X_1 and W for each individual must be equal, and further, it will also equal the ratio of their respective full marginal costs, as in:

$$(5\text{--}9)$$

$$(MRS_{X_1 W})^i = \frac{\partial U^i/\partial X_{1i}}{\partial U^i/\partial W_i} = \frac{\partial C/\partial X_1}{\partial C/\partial W - 1/\theta \, (\partial U^m/\partial W) - 1/\theta \overset{m\text{-}1}{\underset{i=1}{\Sigma}} \lambda_i \, (\partial U^i/\partial W)}$$

Efficient resource allocation at any point in time implies that each individual's marginal rate of substitution equals the ratio of the marginal costs. The terms with W reflect the congestion externalities associated with such use. Thus, the Pareto-efficient criteria implies that for static resources allocation decisions, use intensity is important. More generally, if one allows the stock of facilities capable of producing W to be augmented, then it becomes clear that these decisions cannot be made without knowlege of the congestion levels and the costs associated with crowding or disruption to solitude. This principle will be operationalized with the already estimated willingness-to-pay functions in subsequent sections.

A SIMPLE MODEL FOR DETERMINING OPTIMAL USE

Wilderness recreationists are primarily concerned with solitude as well as with the primeval setting in which they enjoy hiking, horseback riding, and associated wilderness experiences. To make the empirical model useful for decisionmaking, it is necessary to define a relationship between certain patterns of use and the associated intrusions upon solitude, which have been measured by number of encounters. There are basically three approaches to arrive at such relationships. The first is through experienced judgement. That is, one might specify some assumed functional relationship that might be suggested by the observations of experienced wilderness-area managers. This approach is likely to be of limited value. Wilderness use and the behavioral patterns of recreationists both imply that analytically tractable functions will not provide reasonable descriptions of the underlying process. Therefore, the use of judgment will be even less suitable.

A second approach would call for empirically estimating use-characteristic (i.e., encounter) relationships. The collection of the data necessary for this task represents a significant problem. It would be difficult to tabulate the required data, since one cannot control and hence monitor the movements of recreationists once they are inside a wilderness area. It would, of course, be possible to ask users to maintain a diary or journal of their experiences. However, this would not assure that a full range of total use intensities had been explored, since the researcher would have to rely on these patterns of use of a given area over time. Cross-sectional studies across several wilderness areas are likely to be unsuccessful, since there are great divergences in the characteristics of these areas.

The final approach to the problem of developing a use-encounter relationship is to construct a stochastic simulation model of a wilderness area.[3] The basic data for the model might represent the features of an actual area and its pattern of use. Repeated simulation experiments would allow the researcher to control the "hypothetical recreationists' behavior."

Since the model presented here is illustrative rather than definitive, additional discussion of the issue involved in choosing among these alternative strategies need not be addressed further. They have been reviewed to indicate the further research problems and to indicate that the method selected below has been chosen for illustrative purposes only.

Characteristically, wilderness recreationists participate in wilderness use in groups, and it is the number of these groups or parties in an area at any interval of time that will determine the frequency of encounters. Note, however, that if parties have two rather than four members, there will be significant effects on the total number of users (holding the number of parties constant). But the size of the party is not likely to be an important determinant of the probability of encounters for any individual. It should be noted that the number of individuals in a party may affect the severity of the encounter in terms of the perceived disruption to solitude. Accordingly, some attention must be given to the relationship between parties and users. This relationship will have implications for (a) the encounter-use patterns in a given area; and (b) the number of individuals whose willingness-to-pay functions are affected by congestion.

3. The application of such a model applied to the Spanish Peaks Area is discussed in Smith and Krutilla [6].

Despite the above qualifications, for the following application several simplifying assumptions will be made. The most important of these are: (a) the number of individuals in a party will be assumed to be constant at four;[4] (b) the length of stay or the trip length of party will be assumed to be constant at four days; and (c) the size of the party will be assumed not to influence the disruptive effect of encounters. The first two assumptions concern variables that might have been assumed to be instruments of managerial policy. It will be clear that there is nothing in the analytical model that prevents such a specification. A simplified analysis has been selected deliberately in order to illustrate the usefulness of willingness-to-pay functions for managerial purposes. Such additional qualifications that managers may deem to be important can be readily handled by the methodology. It is further assumed that wilderness management develops optimization plans based upon the typical or average trip. Alternative objective functions for optimization might also be developed in terms of the range of experiences of users (i.e., higher-order moments of the distribution of willingness-to-pay). But each more complicated objective function would require that the use-encounter relationship be more accurately defined that it will be for this example. If the average or typical trip is selected for optimization purposes by management, the expected values of trail and camp encounters are the only moments of the respective probability distributions that need to be considered.

It is assumed that the expected number of trail encounters per day, λ_T, is a function of the total number of parties P, in the area for each day and the physical characteristics of the area. Among these characteristics that are likely to be important are the number of entry points, E; the total number of trail miles, K_1; and the number of trail intersections, I. Equation (5–10) expresses this relationship in general terms.

$$\lambda_T = f(P, E, K_1, I) \tag{5–10}$$

Similarly, the expected number of nights in which there was at least one camp encounter, designated λ_C, is a function of area characteristics. It should be noted that this measure of camp

---

4. The reason for this assumption stems from the questionnaire, which described encounters with backpackers of parties with four or less members. See Appendix A for the questionnaire.

encounters is only one of several that might have been used. It was selected for the survey because it provides a reasonable summary of the distribution of camp encounters over the nights of a trip. Some likely determinants of camp encounters are the number of parties in the area on any given day; the total number of camp sites available, K_2; and the average distance between camp sites, d. Equation (5–11) provides a general specification.

$$\lambda_C = g(P, K_2, d) \tag{5-11}$$

Based upon the assumption that all parties are equal in size, the total number of users, N, is a linear function of the number of parties and can be used to replace P in equations (5–10) and (5–11). Therefore, expected encounters become a function of the level of use (i.e., $N = \phi P$).

The process of aggregation from the individual's willingness-to-pay function to the aggregate schedule can be greatly simplified if it is assumed that all users are alike in their economic and demographic characteristics. Using the semilog specification, the aggregate willingness-to-pay function, AWP, can be represented by:

$$AWP = Ne^{\alpha - \beta Tn - \gamma Cn} \tag{5-12}$$

where

α, β, γ = measured coefficients

Tn = number of trail encounters per day

Cn = number of nights with at least one camp encounter

N = number of individual users

e = base of natural logarithm system

Replacing Tn and Cn by their expected values, λ_T and λ_C, and these values by their respective functions f and g, equation:

$$AWP = Ne^{\alpha - \beta f\left(\frac{1}{\phi}N, E, K_1, I\right) - \gamma g\left(\frac{1}{\phi}N, K_2, d\right)} \tag{5-13}$$

If the management objective is to select the level of use that maximizes aggregate willingness-to-pay, then the appropriate level of use can be selected by maximizing (5–13), with N as a control variable.

$$\frac{d(AWP)}{dN} = e^{[\alpha - \beta\bar{f}(N) - \gamma\bar{g}(N)]} - \left(\beta\frac{d\bar{f}}{dN} + \gamma\frac{d\bar{g}}{dN}\right) AWP = 0 \qquad (5\text{–}14)$$

Equation (5–14) assumes that all other factors are held constant for the area

$$[\text{i.e., } \bar{f}(N) = f\left(\frac{1}{\phi} N, \bar{K}_2, \bar{d}\right)].$$

If the first derivatives of f and g are not functions of N, solution for the optimal level of use from (5–14) is straightforward. Equation (5–15) provides the solution when df/dN and dg/dN are constants θ_1 and θ_2, respectively.

$$N^* = \frac{1}{\beta\theta_1 + \gamma\theta_2} \qquad (5\text{–}15)$$

More complex specifications of f and g will, of course, make the solution less straightforward. Several observations should be made regarding Equation (5–14). The first term measures the contribution to aggregate WP from one additional user, and the second measures the loss to all other users as a result of that marginal user's entry into the system. There is a maximum AWP when the marginal contribution to benefits is exactly offset by the marginal impact on congestion costs.

For given values of θ_1 and θ_2 the optimal level of daily use can be derived. However, at present such parameters are unknown, and the best one might come up with would be mere guesses. For example, when f and g are given by (5–16) and (5–17):

$$\bar{f}(N) = \theta_1 N \qquad (5\text{–}16)$$

$$\bar{g}(N) = \theta_2 N \qquad (5\text{–}17)$$

one method of deriving parameter values would be to set θ_1 and θ_2 to conform approximately to present use-encounter patterns at the Spanish Peaks Primitive Area (i.e., $\theta_1 = 0.02$ and $\theta_2 = 0.015$). If it is further assumed that backpackers use the area the optimal daily level of use can be derived. It would equal approximately two hundred individuals, or fifty parties each with four members. This calculation is simply illustrative and depends on the estimated willingness-to-pay function used and the parametric form of (5–16) and (5–17).

While it was argued earlier that the levels of willingness-to-pay predicted by the estimated willingness-to-pay relationship cannot be considered to indicate the "true" level of willingness-to-pay, these levels can be used to illustrate how management might determine the optimal level of use. Using the OLS estimate of the willingness-to-pay function (encounters with backpackers), the mean values for all regressors except trail encounters and camp encounters, and assuming that the length of trip is four days, Equation (5–18) can be derived.

$$\log (WBP) = 2.578 - 0.114Tn - 0.211Cn \tag{5–18}$$

where:

WBP = willingness-to-pay for encounters with backpacking parties

Tn = average number of trail encounters per day

Cn = number of nights with at least one camp encounter

Table 5.1 presents an example that uses this relationship together with (5–16) and (5–17) to determine the optimal level of use of the facility, assuming the season is sixty days in length. This example illustrates that a policy which seeks to maximize the net benefits to users of a wilderness area must trade off two opposing effects. Increasing the total level of use, from 150 to 250 in our example, allows more individuals to enjoy the area. However, the quality of each individual's experience declines because of the congestion effects resulting from increased use. Accordingly it is not then surprising to find seasonal AWP to be less with 250 users. Our rather simple example indicates that 200 users per day would be optimal.

Table 5-1. An Example of the Determination of Optimal Total Use

Level of Daily Use (N)	Expected Daily Trail Encounters	Expected Number of Nights of Camp Encounters	Season AWP
150[a]	3	2.25	$13,650[b]
100	4	3	$14,170
250[a]	5	3.75	$11,970

[a]The values of nights of camp encounters have been rounded to the nearest integer value for the calculation of season *AWP*.

[b]These values understate the expected willingness-to-pay since the expected value of the antilog of the predictions from equation (5-18) will be less than the antilog of the expected value.

It should be clear that this example has no direct implications for the Spanish Peaks Area. Rather it serves to illustrate how the information from quality-adjusted willingness-to-pay relationships might be used in managing wilderness areas.

CONGESTION AND RESOURCE ALLOCATION: AN ADAPTED HELLS CANYON MODEL

Direct measurement of the benefits associated with the preservation of natural environments, which provide amenity services that do not exchange in the market, in most studies has been an elusive problem. Since many of these resources have unique natural attributes, they can be effectively considered irreplaceable and irreproducible. Fisher, Krutilla, and Cicchetti [3] have recently discussed the key components of the economics of preservation versus development in such cases. Their model assumes that one can quantify (at least in an approximate sense) the forces that cause the preservation benefits to increase over time.[5] The willingness-to-pay for these amenity services is hypothesized to increase as a result of growth in demand. Technical change will result in a growth in income which, given the absence of good substitutes for these services and relatively high income elasticities, will cause the willingness-to-pay to increase.[6]

In addition, an expected population growth, increasing demand

5. The model is developed in more detail in Krutilla and Cicchetti [4].
6. Smith [5] provides a derivation of the specific conditions required for relative price change.

derived from "learning by doing," and a variety of similar forces will cause quantity demanded at zero price to increase. Accordingly, the demand for the amenity services provided by natural environments is likely to be shifting outward from the origin over time, as shown in Figure 5.1. Since the supply of natural endowments that provide these services is fixed, and the quality of the services remains constant, their relative price must rise as their relative scarcity increases. In terms of Figure 5.1 the vertical shift P_0P_1 results from the growth in income associated with technical change, as well as from any bias in the incidence of that technological innovation. In

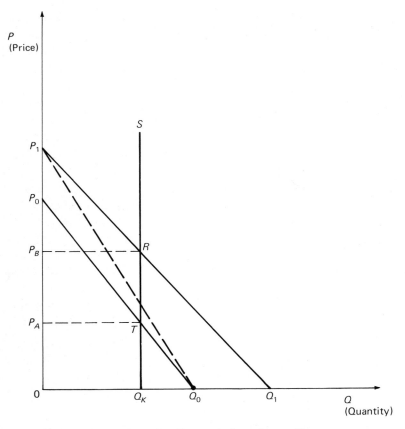

Figure 5–1. Changing Demands for a Scarce Resource.

the absence of horizontal growth, the demand in period one would be $P_1 Q_0$ as compared with $P_0 Q_0$ in period zero. As noted, however, there are forces which can be expected to increase the quantity demand at zero price to, say, Q_1. If the supply of constant quality amenity services from natural endowments is fixed, then it might be expected that markets would ration them through increased prices such as $0P_A$ and $0P_B$ for periods zero and one, respectively.

The Krutilla-Cicchetti [4] model assumes that it may be easier to determine how the demand for amenity services is changing over time than to assign a value to those services at any point in time. Thus, if it is assumed that a measure of consumer's surplus will be used to evaluate benefits—such as the area under $P_0 Q_0$ over the relevant region—then it may be possible to describe how these benefits will change over time. That is, assume that the demand for amenity services can be reasonably approximated by a linear function, and that one can specify a range of values for the rate of shifting of the vertical and horizontal intercept, then one can determine the resulting rate of change in the measured benefits.[7] By assuming the initial benefits (area under the demand curve) to be one dollar, measuring the stream of benefits resulting from growth in demand, and calculating the present value of that stream, it is possible to determine what the initial value of preservation would need to be in order to just offset the development alternative. That is, without specific knowledge of the current benefits derived from the amenity services enjoyed at a preserved natural area, this model provides a means of assessing what these benefits would have to be for given growth rates to have a present value equivalent to that of the development alternative.

The results are, of course, sensitive to the selection of the parameters involved. A series of sensitivity experiments performed by Krutilla and Cicchetti suggest that two parameters are quite important. These are the rate of growth in the vertical intercept, and the definition of capacity (i.e., Q_K in Figure 5.1). The first parameter of these has been investigated by Smith [5]. His research indicated that the rate of relative price appreciation can be related to the rate of technological change, as well as parameters describing the character of preferences and of supply. The second parameter concerns the definition of constant quality service flows and the ability of each natural area to provide them.

7. See Cicchetti's appendix to the Krutilla and Cicchetti [4] paper.

It is possible to adapt the Krutilla-Cicchetti Hells Canyon model so that congestion adjustment is also reflected in the growth in demand for amenity services. Consider that model again. In Figure 5.2 the initial market demand is assumed to be $D_1 D_1'$. Assume that the forces of technological change and population growth, as well as other factors, cause a shift in demand in the next period to $D_2 D_2'$. If the price for these services remains at zero, total use will increase by $D_1' D_2'$. Under the original model this effect would be important only to the extent that it resulted in use exceeding a capacity constraint (Q_K in Figure 5.1). For the present purposes this notion

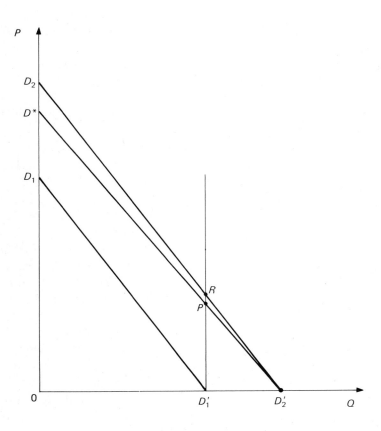

Figure 5-2. Congestion Adjusted Demand Schedule.

will be generalized. Note that there is an array of use densities, and each level of use above $0D_1'$ has a different quality associated with it.

Fisher and Krutilla [2] have employed the same notion in defining a special set of aggregate demand schedules—one for each use intensity. They assumed for diagrammatic simplicity that there were threshold levels of use separating each demand schedule. Clearly this assumption can be relaxed (they do so in later analysis) and this corresponds to the present model in which total use in excess of $0D_1'$ changes the quality of the wilderness experience.

The willingness-to-pay schedules, whose definitions and estimates were presented in previous chapters, provide the means of associating congestion and price or willingness-to-pay. With increased use, the encounters, which an individual can expect to have during the course of the trip, increase. These encounters represent disruptions to solitude and therefore reductions in the quality of the experience. Hence, with knowledge of the relationship between use level and encounters, and the manner in which total use is to increase over time, then it is possible to adjust benefit estimates for congestion. Moreover, an optimal carrying capacity can be defined using the type of analysis discussed in the previous section.

Aggregate willingness-to-pay is maximized when the benefits associated with an additional user are just equal to the losses resulting from the increase in congestion caused by that user [see equation (5–14)]. In terms of Figure 5.2, the benefits associated solely with an increase in use from $0D_1'$ to $0D_2'$ are given by $D_1' RD_2'$. If it is assumed that congestion affects the willingness-to-pay of each individual for wilderness experiences at each level of use without influencing the quantity demanded, as the estimated willingness-to-pay functions suggest, then increased congestion serves to shift $D_2 D_2'$ about the point D_2'. Assuming for the purpose of the example that the congestion resulting from an increase of $D_1' D_2'$ is measured by the shift from $D_2 D_2'$ to $D^* D_2'$, then the congestion losses are given by $D_2 D_2' D^*$.

This marginal comparison amounts to comparing $D_1' PD_2'$ to $PRD_2 D^*$, since $PD_2' R$ is a common area to both. Assume the managerial objective is to maximize aggregate willingness-to-pay, and further that the administrative and ecological costs associated with increased use are assumed to be negligible.[8] This analysis shows that

8. Fisher and Krutilla [2] develop a general framework in which administrative and ecological costs are also important to the definition of carrying capacity.

the carrying capacity of an area can be defined as the total service flow that satisfies this equality condition between increments to the benefits from increased use relative to the increments to congestion costs associated with that increase in use.

As noted above, these demand functions are not generally known for amenity services, so that the relevance of this adjustment to the Hells Canyon model lies in its effects on the growth in the benefits, and therefore the initial year's preservation benefits, required to be indifferent between preservation and development of the resource. The logic underlying this statement is straightforward. If one knows the determinants of the growth in demand for amenity services and their approximate effects in terms of a linear schedule, the growth rate for the benefits can be determined.[9] By assigning some initial value to the benefits of the first year, such as one dollar, it is possible to define the present value of a benefit stream starting from this base, with a varying growth rate determined by the parametric assumptions about demand. If this present value is compared with the benefits from development, it is possible to define the question: What do the initial preservation benefits would *have to be* in order to be indifferent between the mutually inconsistent preservation and development alternatives?

A comparison of this value with the best estimates of the benefits from providing such amenity services in the current year permits the policymaker to decide whether preservation or development is in the highest social interest.[10] It will be sensitive to the parametric assumptions and the defined capacity constraint. Table 5.2 illustrates this sensitivity with the assumption that capacity is achieved in the first year. Benefits are measured once capacity is reached *as if* price rationing were used. In terms of Figure 5.1, this means that a capacity of Q_K implies benefits in year zero of $0P_0TQ_K$ and in year one of $0P_1RQ_K$. Prices of $0P_A$ and $0P_B$ ration use to the level of constant-quality services—Q_K. This procedure assumes that Q_K is defined exogenously. Information on the congestion effects permits one to define Q_K endogenously. For example, in Table 5.2, if the vertical growth in price proceeds at 4 percent annually, and the horizontal growth in quantity at 10 percent, the initial preservation benefits required to be indifferent between preservation and

9. See Krutilla and Cicchetti [4], pp. 25–28.
10. For an example of the use of the methodology see Fisher, Krutilla, and Cicchetti [3].

Table 5-2. Initial Year's Preservation Benefits Required for Each $1 million of Present Value of Development Benefits[a]

		Annual Growth in Demand at Zero Price (horizontal shift)		
Annual Growth in to Pay at Zero Quantity (vertical shift)		7.5%	10%	12%
	3%	$44,442	$42,572	$41,186
	4%	37,200	35,662	34,535
	5%	30,172	28,964	28,096

[a]The assumptions underlying these calculations are: (1) interest rate is 10%; (2) capacity achieved at year 1; (3) growth in quantity demanded reduces to population growth at 50 years.

development is $35,662 for $1 million of development benefits (in present value terms).[11]

The empirical estimates of the effect of congestion on willingness-to-pay can be used to define the capacity constraint for the Spanish Peaks. Once again, however, it is necessary to make some rather arbitrary assumptions regarding the use-encounter relationship. Consider the semilog specification of the willingness-to-pay relationship. This relationship indicates that there are diminishing marginal effects for encounters. The coefficient of trail encounters can be interpreted as follows:

$$a_{TN} = \frac{\partial WP/\partial TN}{WP} = \frac{\partial WP/WP}{\partial TN} \qquad (5\text{-}19)$$

where

TN = trail encounters

WP = willingness-to-pay

A change in the total level of use affects the perceived congestion and therefore the willingness-to-pay. For purposes of simplicity, assume that only trail encounters are relevant and that camp

11. The model has been tested for the sensitivity of this assumption, and the middle case (i.e., 10 percent horizontal, 4 percent vertical) under alternative interest rate assumptions. For example, with 7 percent this benefit requirement is $16,832, while with 13 percent it is $55,168.

encounters can be translated into an equivalent number of trail encounters. Additionally, assume that attention will focus on encounters with hiking parties and that horseback encounters can be translated into an equivalent number of backpacking encounters. Equation (5–20) provides a simple statement of the relationship between the change in total use (X) and encounters (TN).

$$\frac{\partial WP/WP}{\partial X} = \frac{1}{WP}\left(\frac{\partial WP}{\partial X}\right) = \frac{1}{WP}\left(\frac{\partial WP}{\partial TN}\right)\left(\frac{\partial TN}{\partial X}\right) = a_{TN}\left(\frac{\partial TN}{\partial X}\right) \qquad (5–20)$$

Moreover, is use is increasing over time, the change in WP due to congestion costs may be expressed as:

$$\frac{\partial WP/WP}{\partial t} = \frac{1}{WP}\left(\frac{\partial WP}{\partial t}\right) = \frac{1}{WP}\left(\frac{\partial WP}{\partial TN}\right)\left(\frac{\partial TN}{\partial X}\right)\left(\frac{\partial X}{\partial t}\right) = a_{TN}\left(\frac{\partial TN}{\partial t}\right) \quad (5–21)$$

An important parameter is unknown. It is the change in trail encounters with respect to use, or alternatively stated, the change in trail encounters over time. For the purpose of illustration this parameter $\partial TN/\partial t$ has been approximated using an arbitrarily defined Taylor expansion in t (specifically the first three terms). Several scenarios were analyzed. They differed in part because various rates of growth in price and quantity were considered. Table 5.3 presents the results for the middle case (i.e., 4 percent vertical shift and 10 percent horizontal shift). Bracketed GLS estimates of the effect of trail encounters on WP have been examined. The preceding equations indicate the importance of the change in encounters over time. For descriptive purposes each case is classified according to the initial level of this change in encounters with time, as well as the rate at which this rate changes over time (i.e., they are analogous to the value of the first derivative and the second derivative, respectively). The specific details of this function and the other parameters are discussed below.

The values in Table 5.3 are comparable to those of 5.2 in that they also report the initial year's breakeven preservation benefits for each million dollars of present value of development benefits. The numbers in parentheses below the dollar estimates are the years in which capacity is reached and price is assumed to ration use as in the original model. One conclusion is that this extension of the

Table 5-3. Preservation Benefits Required for Each $1 Million of Present Value of Development Benefits — Variation in Quality and Prices to Ration Services[a]

Growth in Encounters		*Congestion* −0.054	*Effect* −0.114
Initial Year	*Rate of Increase*		
Low	Low	$27,414 (5)	$29,264 (4)
	Medium	29,195 (4)	31,166 (3)
	High	31,077 (3)	31,231 (3)
Medium	Low	29,190 (4)	31,266 (3)
	Medium	29,302 (4)	31,330 (3)
	High	31,154 (3)	33,355 (2)
High	Low	29,298 (4)	31,440 (3)
	Medium	31,201 (3)	33,444 (2)
	High	31,232 (3)	33,444 (2)

[a] The assumptions underlying these calculations are: (1) interest rate is 10%; (2) annual growth in quantity demanded at zero price is 10%; (3) annual growth in willingness-to-pay at zero quantity is 4%.

Krutilla-Cicchetti computational model significantly reduces the breakeven value for the preservation benefits.[12]

12. All three values of possible interest rates were investigated. The sensitivity is seen as follows ($\alpha = -0.054$)

		Interest Rate	
Vertical = 4%		7%	13%
Horizontal = 10%			
Growth in Encounters			
Level	*Rate*		
Low	Low	$12,391 (5)	$43,902 (5)
High	High	$14,453 (3)	$49,092 (3)

If the horizontal shifter is allowed to change with, $a = -0.054$ and interest rate at 10 percent we have:

A SENSITIVITY ANALYSIS OF THE EXPANDED
HELLS CANYON MODEL

The results presented in the previous section are sensitive to the magnitudes of parameters specified for the demand growth, the growth in encounters, the discount rate, and the measured effect of encounter willingness-to-pay. If one were to consider variations in any one or more of these factors, the resulting variations in Tables 5.2 and 5.3 become so extensive that it would be difficult to summarize their overall meaning. Yet it is clear that any one specification of the model is overly restrictive. It is important to isolate which variables have the most significant impact on such breakeven analysis.

One method of summarizing these effects is to perform a multivariate statistical analysis to summarize the relationship between the factors describing the alternative scenarios and the response—namely the present value of a benefit stream with initial value of one dollar. It should be emphasized that a particular solution is not important; instead, the objective is to summarize the responses from a number of scenarios or specifications of the parameters involved for the purpose of learning what is important, rather than to test specific hypotheses. Finally, because the model is not stochastic, probability statements regarding the estimated effects of one variable relative to another are not appropriate.

Multiple-regression analysis was selected to summarize the cases in which the model was applied. Seven factors were varied. They include (1) the rate of growth in the vertical intercept of a linear demand schedule (i.e., the rate of increase in prices); (2) the rate of growth in the horizontal intercept or the increase in quantity demanded at zero price; (3) the rate of discount utilized in calculating the present value; (4) the three coefficients for the Taylor expansion to determine growth in encounters for a given growth in quantity demanded; and (5) the parameter used to measure effect of en-

		Horizontal Shifter	
Level	*Rate*	7.5%	12.5%
Low	Low	$32,195	$24,573
		(4)	(5)
High	High	$33,867	$29,110
		(3)	(3)

counters on willingness-to-pay. Three variations of each of these factors were considered implying that 2,187 separate scenarios were developed. These were summarized with respect to their effect on the present value calculation using a regression analysis. Table 5.4 presents these parametric variations in detail. Equation (5–22) provides the estimated summary equation in linear form for the 2,187 cases. The dependent variable is the present value, *PV*, of the benefit stream, with an initial year's value of one dollar.

$$\bar{PV} = 77.883 + 1315.767X_R + 171.249X_G - 935.847X_I \quad (5\text{–}22)$$
$$(2.731) \quad\quad (34.384) \quad\quad (13.754) \quad\quad (11.461)$$

$$+ \ 65.139 \ X_\beta - 54.852X_{\alpha_0} + 60.483X_{\alpha_1} - 97.383X_{\alpha_2}$$
$$(9.551) \quad\quad (13.754) \quad\quad (34.384) \quad\quad (34.384)$$

$$S = 13.129$$
$$R^2 = 0.793$$

The value in parentheses below the estimated coefficients are the standard errors. The signs for all variables conform to what was expected to happen with variations in any particular variable. For example, increases in the discount rate (X_I) will reduce the present value. An increase in the discount rate of 1 percent (absolute value) reduces the present value of the benefit stream by about $9.36. Increases in the absolute magnitude of congestion decreases the present value, since X_β is entered in a negative form, etc.

The results suggest that the output of the model in terms of the initial year's benefits from preservation required to offset the development alternative is sensitive to the specification of the model. Two of the primary components of the specification have been linked to variables on which additional research may be able to collect more information. Smith's [5] research on the determinants of relative price change in the presence of technical change provides alternative models for determining the magnitude of the vertical shift in demand. The present empirical research enables one to overcome the arbitrary definition of a capacity constraint, but it does require the measurement of a total use-encounter relationship. Additional work in this area will help remove some of the more important qualifications made in both the static and dynamic case studies reviewed in this chapter.

Table 5–4. Design Points for the Congestion Scenarios

Variable	*Values*		
(1) Annual Growth in Willingness to Pay at Zero Quantity Demanded (vertical shift) (X_R)	3 %	4%	5 %
(2) Annual Growth in Quantity Demanded at Zero Price (horizontal shift) (X_G)	7.5%	10%	12.5%
(3) Interest Rate for (X_I) Discounting	7 %	10%	13 %
(4) Measured Effect of encounters on Willingness to Pay $(X_\beta)^a$	−0.047	−0.083	−0.119
(5) $\alpha_0{}^b$ (X_{α_0})	.025	.050	.075
(6) α_1 (X_{α_1})	.000	− .010	− .020
(7) α_2 (X_{α_2})	.020	.030	.040

[a]These values represent the GLS estimates of the effect of trail encounters on willingness-to-pay and the end points of a 95 per cent confidence interval for the estimated effect.

[b]The specification of the encounter growth is given as:

$$\frac{\partial TN}{\partial t} = \alpha_0 + \alpha_1 t + \alpha_2 t^2$$

The values of α_0, α_1, and α_2 are adjusted further by the values of the annual growth in quantity demanded to reflect increases with high levels of growth and decreases for lower levels.

SUMMARY AND CONCLUSIONS

Willingness-to-pay functions adjusted for quality are a variant of the hedonic approach of constructing price indexes that can be used to analyze quality differences. In this chapter their usefulness was illustrated for static resource allocation management decisions as well as dynamic investment decisions. In the first instance natural areas providing amenity services whose quality is deleteriously affected by congestion were considered. In the second, problems associated with investment decisions for natural environments among alternative, mutually exclusive uses were studied. Some of the specific findings can now be summarized.

1. Pareto-efficient resource allocation requires that the congestion externalities associated with high levels of use be reflected in the

marginal costs for the purpose of optimum resource allocation. That is, a Pareto-efficient allocation of resources—between the production of a good that is subject to congestion externalities and one that is not—calls for equating the marginal rate of substitution in consumption for these goods to the ratio of the congestion-adjusted marginal costs for all individuals.

2. Since congestion may serve to diminish the quality of the services provided by wilderness recreation, it follows that increasing the levels of use of a fixed set of natural areas will not necessarily be synonymous with increasing the benefits resulting from these activities. A simple model that calls for maximization of the aggregate willingness-to-pay of wilderness users of a given area indicates that total use should be allowed to increase only to the level of use where the increment to benefits from that additional use is just offset by the congestion costs imposed on others (assuming, of course, there are no other costs associated with the increase in use).

3. Efficient resource allocation requires that each resource input be allocated to its highest valued use. It has been difficult to determine measures of the value of amenity services. While some efforts have succeeded—notably the travel-cost model (see Cicchetti, Fisher and Smith [1] for a review)—an adjustment for quality has not generally been possible. An alternative approach developed by Krutilla and Cicchetti [4] develops a model to measure the rate of growth in benefits over time in order to determine what the initial year's benefits, given this predetermined rate of growth, would need to be in order to be indifferent between alternative preservation and development uses. This approach is sensitive to a number of key assumptions, one of which—the capacity of an area to provide constant quality services—can be relaxed using the quality-adjusted willingness-to-pay functions, as the second application discussed in this chapter indicates.

4. The revised methodology developed, which permits the recreational carrying capacity of an area to be endogenously defined, is nonetheless sensitive to the particular values of the parameters selected. Based upon an analysis of 2,187 independent scenarios, it can be concluded that all factors have important effects. Therefore, the specification of their values must be based on each area's unique situation.

REFERENCES

1. C.J. Cicchetti, A.C. Fisher, and V.K. Smith, "Economic Models and Planning Outdoor Recreation," *Operations Research* 21 (September/October 1973).

2. A.C. Fisher and J.V. Krutilla, "Determination of Optimal Capacity of Resource-Based Recreation Facilities," *Natural Resources Journal* 12 (July 1972).

3. A.C. Fisher, J.V. Krutilla, and C.J. Cicchetti, "The Economics of Environmental Preservation: A Theoretical and Empirical Analysis," *American Economic Review* 62 (September 1972).

4. J.V. Krutilla and C.J. Cicchetti, "Evaluating Benefits of Environmental Resources with Special Application to the Hells Canyon," *Natural Resources Journal* 12 (January 1972).

5. V.K. Smith, *Technical Change, Relative Prices, and Environmental Resource Evaluation* (Baltimore: Johns Hopkins Univeristy Press, 1974).

6. V.K. Smith and J.V. Krutilla, *The Structure and Properties of a Wilderness Users Travel Simulator: With Special Application to the Spanish Peaks Area* (Baltimore: Johns Hopkins University, 1976).

Chapter Six

The Costs of Congestion:
A Capsule Summary

The economic analysis of externalities has developed from the study of largely irrelevant and whimsical examples, such as the bees and nectar fable, to become the focal point of the literature of environmental economics. The problems of pollution and congestion are now recognized as among the most challenging for the efficient allocation of resources. The purpose of this book has been to develop a methodology for measuring the effects of congestion so that the costs associated with it might be taken into account in public allocation decisions.

Conventional economic analysis of the consumer choice problem largely assumes away congestion by postulating a model in which the individual consumes goods and services of given quality. It is difficult to integrate the effects of congestion into this framework. The use of the time costs associated with waiting as a result of congestion is one attempt to reflect the implications of high-use intensity patterns. However, as noted above, crowding can have a variety of effects, only a few of which are associated with time. They range from the litter and available space for sunbathing on a public beach to the ecological damage to a natural habitat.

In attempting to account for all the dimensions of the congestion problem, three models of consumer behavior were reviewed: (1) the conventional model, where congestion is treated as another good; (2) the consumers-as-producers model, where congestion affects the individual's ability to produce homogeneous final service flows; and (3) the Lancaster [3] model, where congestion affects the attributes available from certain goods or services. It was then concluded that the measurement of the effects of crowding must therefore proceed:

(1) to define appropriate measures of the effects of congestion on the goods and services of interest; (2) to quantify these measures in a means that allows individuals to evaluate their implications; (3) to evaluate the effects of any level of total use on the congestion measure; and (4) to convert these changes into value terms.

These objectives are difficult to fully accomplish. However, it is possible to take some reasonable first steps in a rough-and-ready way when the characteristics of the good or service are well defined. For the problem area considered—wilderness recreation—the primary concern of the recreationist is solitude. Accordingly, intrusion upon the perceived solitude will reduce the vector of attributes that may fully describe the solitude parameter. The survey research of George Stankey [6] has been particularly helpful, since his findings suggest that encounters with other parties provide a reasonably good measure of these disruptions of solitude. As Fisher and Krutilla [1] have noted, different types of encounters in different circumstances are likely to have differential impacts on an individual's utility. Encounters on the trailhead (i.e., at the outset of the trip) may be less distasteful, since they are anticipated by the user. Meetings after a one- or two-day trek into the center of a wilderness area, however, may be quite disruptive. Additionally, the size and mode of travel of the party encountered are also likely to be important to the perceived disruption of solitude.

Careful enumeration of all the possible factors influencing the severity of the effect of an encounter would reveal a very large design space. While it is true that encounters have been shown to affect the satisfaction of wilderness users,[1] there was not, prior to this analysis, an established link between these quality variables and an individual's revealed willingness-to-pay. Thus it is reasonable to test some fairly simple hypotheses with the most powerful statistical tools available, and to proceed to further refinements when necessary.

By using a sample of wilderness users of the Spanish Peaks Primitive Area and a set of hypothetical experiences that considered the minimum possible refinement to the definition of the encounter scenario, the problem was still difficult. Each of the possible scenarios could not be asked of each sample respondent with a mail interview questionnaire. Both the response rate and the accuracy of any respondent's answers will be related to the length of the ques-

---

1. See Fisher and Krutilla [1] and Stankey [6] for further discussion.

tionnaire. Thus there was a need to reduce the set of questions asked of any individual to a more manageable number. Such a reduction was accomplished using the principles of experimental design, given a rather diffuse prior expectation as to the functional form of the willingness-to-pay function. Each individual received a random sample from the possible questions. Since the probability of any question being asked for any individual was equal across all individuals, it was assured that there would be an approximately equal number of responses for each scenario. Approximately 600 questionnaires were mailed to a sample of 1970 summer users of the Spanish Peaks. The sample was selected by Robert Lucas and George Stankey.

Over 40 percent of the individuals responded after two mailings. Some of these were necessarily omitted because the respondents did not or could not answer the questions as posed to them.[2] The remainder, a total of one hundred and ninety-five individuals, formed the basis of the empirical analysis, which was undertaken in two phases. A variety of functional specifications, that were admissible on the basis of economic theory were tested, including linear and semilog formats. Within the linear specification, tests were performed for linear and nonlinear effects of both the encounters and socio-economic variables. These results suggested that encounters did, in fact, have an important effect on willingness-to-pay. There was not, however, a statistically significant difference in the estimated effects for trail encounters versus nights in which there was at least one camp encounter.

Since five hypothetical experiences were solicited of each individual, it was possible to estimate the relative variation in the ordinary least-squares (OLS) residuals (i.e., the difference between the predicted and actual values for the relevant dependent variable), and to determine whether or not the informational content, in terms of each individual's response set, differed across the sample. The findings suggest wide variations, so an estimating technique that utilized this additional information was necessary. Consequently a generalized least-squares (GLS) estimator was used to estimate the acceptable linear and semilog specifications. The results suggest dramatic increases in the efficiency of estimation.

Two examples were selected to illustrate the use of these empirical

2. The statistical effects of this discrimination have been examined and the results are discussed in Chapter 3.

results in the management and allocation of wilderness and wildlands resources. The first was a simple static model for determining the optimal level of use for the Spanish Peaks Primitive Area, assuming one knows the technical relationship between total use and the expected number of the alternative types of encounters. The second example was dynamic and resulted in a revision of the Krutilla-Cicchetti [2] valuation model for natural endowments, in which the capacity constraint may be determined endogenously using the measured congestion effects from the willingness-to-pay functions. Over two thousand specifications of the model have been considered, and their effects on the present value of benefit stream have been summarized with a multiple-regression equation.

The overall findings of this research suggest that it is possible to measure nontime-related congestion effects. Moreover, the sensitivity analysis indicates that such measures are essential for the efficient management (static) and allocation (dynamic) of "open access" environmental resources. These conclusions, while encouraging, also serve to indicate the need for continued research in this area.

As already noted there are several areas that require more extensive research effort. The first is the modeling and measurement of the effects of total use on those attributes that indicate disruptions of solitude. As suggested, informed judgment and conventional statistical techniques are not likely to be very successful in addressing this problem. It amounts to modeling an extremely complex production process, in economist's jargon, where both quality and quantity must be distinguished. There are no global controls on the system, but rather the process is one in which the open-access facility is used by a variety of individuals at each one's discretion. Continued research by Smith, Webster, and Heck [5] and Smith and Krutilla [4] has resulted in the development of a large-scale traffic simulation model of the process, which may serve to provide the required technical data on use patterns and the associated expected levels of encounters.

A further problem concerns the multiple use of existing facilities. In the case of a wilderness area both backpacking parties and horsepack parties can utilize a given facilty. The economic carrying capacity of an area may need to be defined for each group according to the activity being undertaken. The examples considered above have assumed either a single-use pattern, or have assumed that, in those cases of multiple-use patterns, all other forms of use can be readily transformed to a common *numeraire*. This assumption may be intolerable, and for the purposes of rationing policy it may be necessary to generalize further the definition of carrying capacity.[3]

Further refinements in the definition and measurement of encounters and in the measurement of willingness-to-pay also appear to be necessary. Testing the estimated relationships across different areas in an effort to define user groups with different tolerances for solitude disruptions is another research topic that this study indicates will be fruitful.

As noted at the outset, the allocation problems associated with natural endowments are particularly challenging, and they will require comprehensive analyses of quality-adjusted demand schedules such as that which has been developed in this book. We attempted to develop a new methodology based upon the principles of applied welfare economics. It was never meant to solve the problems of wilderness managers and policymakers in general. Instead its goal is the more modest one of providing such decisionmakers with improved toos for analysis.

REFERENCES

1. A.C. Fisher and J.V. Krutilla, "Determination of Optimal Capacity of Resource-Based Recreation Facilities," *Natural Resources Journal* 12 (July 1972).

2. J.V. Krutilla and C.J. Cicchetti, "Evaluating Benefits of Environmental Resources with Special Application to the Hells Canyon," *Natural Resources Journal* 12 (January 1972).

3. K.J. Lancaster, "A New Approach to Consumer Theory," *Journal of Political Economy* 74 (April 1966).

4. V.K. Smith and J.V. Krutilla, *The Structure and Properties of a Wilderness User's Travel Simulator: With Special Application to the Spanish Peaks Area* (Baltimore: Johns Hopkins University Press, 1976)

5. V.K. Smith, D. Webster, and N. Heck, "A Prototype Simulation Model of a Wilderness Area," *Operational Research Quarterly* (December 1974).

6. G.H. Stankey, "A Strategy for the Definition and Management of Wilderness Quality," in *Natural Environments: Studies in Theoretical and Applied Analysis*, ed. J.V. Krutilla (Baltimore: Johns Hopkins University Press, 1972).

3. Timothy Deyak, at the State Univeristy of New York, Binghamton, is currently investigating this problem with an extended consumer-choice model.

Appendix A

Survey Materials

LETTER WITH FIRST MAILING

The Wilderness Society—729 Fifteenth Street,
N.W., Washington, D.C. 20005

Dear Wilderness User:

Those of us who have enjoyed the wilderness experience know that wilderness areas are often fragile and must be carefully protected from overuse by those of us who are most appreciative of the many values of wilderness.

I hope you will give your careful attention to the enclosed questionnaire on this important matter. This has been prepared by John Krutilla, Director of the Natural Environments Program for Resources for the Future, to gain much-needed information from individuals on their reactions to the wilderness experience. The Wilderness Society is convinced that more information on the distribution of users is needed in order to adequately protect wilderness and to determine levels of human carrying capacity that can be supported without destruction of wild environments or their communities of plants and animals.

We'll be grateful for your help.

Sincerely,
[Signed]
Stewart M. Brandborg
Executive Director

LETTER WITH FIRST MAILING

Resources for the Future, Inc., 1755 Massachusetts
Avenue, N.W., Washington, D.C. 20006

Dear Wilderness User:

The recreational use of wilderness has been increasing rapidly for the last 25 years, but the area designated as wilderness has remained almost unchanged. As a consequence, problems of overuse and damage to the wilderness resource have become more serious.

The Wilderness management agencies (the Forest Service, the National Park Service, the Bureau of Sports Fisheries and Wildlife) are up against difficult questions in dealing with these problems. You helped answer some of these questions by cooperating in the survey of visitors to the Spanish Peaks Primitive Area. Resources for the Future is cooperating with the Forest Service in an extension of the Spanish Peaks study, and we would like to ask you to help one more time.

Information on the value of wilderness recreation is essential, but almost completely lacking now. How much money should agencies invest in managing and protecting wilderness? In areas that are presently not classified as wilderness, how much would the preservation of the area as wilderness be worth compared to other possible uses? Does increasing use reach a point where the value of the experience is pushed down so much that everybody loses more than the additional visitors gain?

One of the reasons no one has ever tried to put a price on wilderness recreation is because it seems "priceless." Most of us feel this way to some extent. However, we do pay for the activity in certain ways; equipment, food, travel to the area, perhaps licenses, guides, and so forth.

The enclosed questionnaire is an experiment intended to provide some notion of how much people might be willing to pay in order to insure themselves of a certain type of wilderness experience. We realize this is a difficult question, but your answers may help protect wilderness for the future. Stewart Brandborg, the executive director of the Wilderness Society, has given the study his support and a letter from him is enclosed.

UNIVERSITY OF PITTSBURGH LIBRARY
AT BRADFORD

Studying what visitors would be willing to pay for a wilderness experience *in no way* means that a charge for visiting wilderness is about to be put into effect. No such plan is even being considered at this time. Fees may be charged some day, but this study is not aimed at that question. Please read the instructions carefully and try to give us your most realistic answers.

INSTRUCTIONS

On any wilderness trip you generally meet some other parties. The number of other parties you encounter and their method of travel (hiking or traveling on horse) usually varies from day to day. The way you feel about seeing these groups may vary according to when you happen to meet them, what they are doing, how many are in the party, and so on.

This questionnaire is designed to find out the highest price you would be willing to pay to control just two of these factors: (1) the number of groups you encounter, and (2) the method of travel (horse or foot) used by these groups. Let us assume that by paying a fee, you could control the number and method of travel of parties you meet each day. The fee covers just yourself; others in your group would have to pay their own. Also assume that the same fees would be charged at all other wildernesses in the U.S.

Some people are more concerned about having other parties camped within sight or sound of their campsite than they are with meeting other parties while on the trail. So, the questions below consider the number of other parties encountered on the trail and the number of nights during which you had others camped near you.

IMAGINE THAT YOU WOULD SPEND A CERTAIN NUMBER OF DAYS IN THE SPANISH PEAKS ON A GIVEN TRIP. WHAT IS THE MOST YOU WOULD BE WILLING TO PAY TO INSURE YOURSELF THE TYPES OF WILDERNESS EXPERIENCES, WHICH ARE DESCRIBED BELOW:

1A   YOUR TRIP IS ——————— DAYS IN LENGTH.
     YOU MEET ——————— OTHER PARTIES ON THE TRAIL
     EACH DAY.
     ALL OF THEM ARE SMALL GROUPS OF HIKERS
     (BACKPACKERS), NOT OVER 4 PEOPLE IN A GROUP.

YOU HAVE OTHER PARTIES CAMPED WITHIN SIGHT OR
SOUND OF YOUR CAMP ——————— NIGHTS. $ ————.——?
(THE HIGHEST PRICE YOU WOULD PAY FOR THE
TRIP—NOT PER DAY)

1B   YOUR TRIP IS ——————— DAYS IN LENGTH.
YOU MEET ——————— OTHER PARTIES ON THE TRAIL
EACH DAY.
ALL OF THEM ARE SMALL GROUPS OF HORSEBACK
TRAVELERS, NOT OVER 4 PEOPLE IN A GROUP, WITH
2 OR 3 PACKHORSES.
YOU HAVE OTHER PARTIES CAMPED WITHIN SIGHT
OR SOUND OF YOUR CAMP ——————— NIGHTS.
$ ————.——? (THE HIGHEST PRICE YOU WOULD PAY
FOR THE TRIP—NOT PER DAY)

2A   YOUR TRIP IS ——————— DAYS IN LENGTH.
YOU MEET ——————— OTHER PARTIES ON THE TRAIL
EACH DAY.
ALL OF THEM ARE SMALL GROUPS OF HIKERS
(BACKPACKERS), NOT OVER 4 PEOPLE IN A GROUP.
YOU HAVE OTHER PARTIES CAMPED WITHIN SIGHT
OR SOUND OF YOUR CAMP ——————— NIGHTS.
$ ————.——? (THE HIGHEST PRICE YOU WOULD PAY
FOR THE TRIP—NOT PER DAY)

2B   YOUR TRIP IS ——————— DAYS IN LENGTH.
YOU MEET ——————— OTHER PARTIES ON THE TRAIL
EACH DAY.
ALL OF THEM ARE SMALL GROUPS OF HORSEBACK
TRAVELERS, NOT OVER 4 PEOPLE IN A GROUP, WITH
2 OR 3 PACKHORSES.
YOU HAVE OTHER PARTIES CAMPED WITHIN SIGHT
OR SOUND OF YOUR CAMP ——————— NIGHTS.
$ ————.——? (THE HIGHEST PRICE YOU WOULD PAY
FOR THE TRIP—NOT PER DAY)

3A   YOUR TRIP IS ——————— DAYS IN LENGTH.
YOU MEET ——————— OTHER PARTIES ON THE TRAIL
EACH DAY.

ALL OF THEM ARE SMALL GROUPS OF HIKERS
(BACKPACKERS), NOT OVER 4 PEOPLE IN A GROUP.
YOU HAVE OTHER PARTIES CAMPED WITHIN SIGHT OR
SOUND OF YOUR CAMP _____ NIGHTS. $ _____.__?
(THE HIGHEST PRICE YOU WOULD PAY FOR THE TRIP
—NOT PER DAY)

3B   YOUR TRIP IS _____ DAYS IN LENGTH.
YOU MEET _____ OTHER PARTIES ON THE TRAIL
EACH DAY.
ALL OF THEM ARE SMALL GROUPS OF HORSEBACK
TRAVELERS, NOT OVER 4 OTHER PARTIES CAMPED
WITHIN SIGHT OR SOUND OF YOUR CAMP _____
NIGHTS. $ _____.__? (THE HIGHEST PRICE YOU
WOULD PAY FOR THE TRIP—NOT PER DAY)

4A   YOUR TRIP IS _____ DAYS IN LENGTH.
YOU MEET _____ OTHER PARTIES ON THE TRAIL
EACH DAY.
ALL OF THEM ARE SMALL GROUPS OF HIKERS
(BACKPACKERS), NO OVER 4 PEOPLE IN A GROUP.
YOU HAVE OTHER PARTIES CAMPED WITHIN SIGHT
OR SOUND OF YOUR CAMP _____ NIGHTS.
$ _____.__? (THE HIGHEST PRICE YOU WOULD PAY
FOR THE TRIP—NOT PER DAY)

4B   YOUR TRIP IS _____ DAYS IN LENGTH.
YOU MEET _____ OTHER PARTIES ON THE TRAIL
EACH DAY.
ALL OF THEM ARE SMALL GROUPS OF HORSEBACK
TRAVELERS, NOT OVER 4 PEOPLE IN A GROUP, WITH
2 OR 3 PACKHORSES.
YOU HAVE OTHER PARTIES CAMPED WITHIN SIGHT
OR SOUND OF YOUR CAMP _____ NIGHTS.
$ _____.__? (THE HIGHEST PRICE YOU WOULD
PAY FOR THE TRIP—NOT PER DAY)

5A   YOUR TRIP IS _____ DAYS IN LENGTH.
YOU MEET _____ OTHER PARTIES ON THE TRAIL
EACH DAY.

ALL OF THEM ARE SMALL GROUPS OF HIKERS
(BACKPACKERS), NOT OVER 4 PEOPLE IN A GROUP.
YOU HAVE OTHER PARTIES CAMPED WITHIN SIGHT
OR SOUND OF YOUR CAMP _____ NIGHTS.
$ _____.___? (THE HIGHEST PRICE YOU WOULD
PAY FOR THE TRIP—NOT PER DAY)

5B   YOUR TRIP IS _____ DAYS IN LENGTH.
YOU MEET _____ OTHER PARTIES ON THE TRAIL
EACH DAY.
ALL OF THEM ARE SMALL GROUPS OF HORSEBACK
TRAVELERS, NOT OVER 4 PEOPLE IN A GROUP, WITH
2 OR 3 PACKHORSES.
YOU HAVE OTHER PARTIES CAMPED WITHIN SIGHT
OR SOUND OF YOUR CAMP _____ NIGHTS.
$ _____.___? (THE HIGHEST PRICE YOU WOULD PAY
FOR THE TRIP—NOT PER DAY)

1. Please estimate your share of the expenses for this wilderness trip
   for the two items below (whether or not you personally paid any
   part of the costs of the trip).

   a. Traveling to and from the wilderness (including meals and
      lodging while traveling) . . . . $ _____

   b. All other expenses (including outfitter's fees, licenses, film,
      food, and equipment bought for camping, hunting, or fishing).
      Do not include the cost of equipment used on previous
      trips. . . . . $ _____

2. What is the highest year of school you have completed? (circle)

   Elementary   High School   College

   1 2 3 4 5 6 7 8   9 10 11 12   13 14 15 16 16+

3. Please check the box that comes closest to your total family
   income before taxes

☐   less than $3,000   ☐ $10,000 up to $15,000
☐ $3,000 up to $5,000   ☐ $15,000 up to $25,000
☐ $5,000 up to $7,000   ☐ $25,000 and over
☐ $7,000 up to $10,000

4. How many weeks of paid vacation does the head of your household receive each year? _____

5. Please check the box that applies to you

     ☐ Male   ☐ Female

6. Your age last birthday? _____

PLEASE MAIL THE COMPLETED QUESTIONNAIRE IN THE ENCLOSED SELF-ADDRESSED ENVELOPE. NO STAMP IS NEEDED: WE HAVE ALREADY PAID THE POSTAGE

<u>THANK YOU VERY MUCH</u>

LETTER WITH SECOND MAILING

Resources for the Future, Inc., 1755 Massachusetts Avenue, N.W., Washington, D.C. 20036

Dear Wilderness User:

A few weeks ago you were mailed a questionnaire the response to which would provide information regarding your attitude toward a number of situations which one could encounter during his travels in the Spanish Peaks Primitive Area. Perhaps this questionnaire failed to get delivered because of the heavy use of the postal facilities during the holidays, or perhaps the press of other activities prevented you from responding at the time.

Since the response of everyone to whom a questionnaire was sent is important to the success of the survey, we are taking the liberty once again to request answers to the questions appearing on the attached questionnaire. If you have recently responded to the original questionnaire, please ignore this reminder.

Note your questionnaire has an identification number. This is included to enable us to keep track of responses. It will not be used in any way to identify respondents.

We will appreciate greatly, your cooperation.

Cordially yours,
[signed]
John V. Krutilla, Director
Natural Environments Program

Appendix B

Aitken Estimation and R^2

Consider equation (B-1) as a linear model with Y a $TX1$ vector, X a TXK matrix, β a $KX1$ vector of parameters, and U a $TX1$ vector of errors.

$$Y = X\beta + U \tag{B-1}$$

In order for R^2 to be interpreted in the conventional manner (i.e., the percent of total variation associated with the estimated relationship), it is necessary that the residuals permit orthogonal partitioning. With OLS and the assumptions of the general linear model [stated in equation (2) of Chapter 3], this can be demonstrated in a straightforward manner.

Consider the case with an Aitken estimator of (B-1). The GLS residuals e, are given as in (B-2), and the sum of squared residuals in (B-3).

$$e = Y - X(X^T\Sigma^{-1} X)^{-1} X^T\Sigma^{-1} Y \tag{B-2}$$

$$e^Te = Y^TY + Y^T \Sigma^{-1}X (X^T\Sigma^{-1}X)^{-1} X^TX (X^T\Sigma^{-1}X)^{-1} X^T\Sigma^{-1} Y \tag{B-3}$$
$$- 2Y^TX(X^T\Sigma^{-1}X)^{-1}X^T\Sigma^{-1} Y$$

The same expression for OLS residuals, ϵ, is given in (B-4).

$$\epsilon^T\epsilon = Y^TY + Y^TX (X^TX)^{-1} X^TX (X^TX)^{-1} X^TY \tag{B-4}$$
$$- 2Y^TX(X^TX)^{-1}X^TY$$

In the case of (B−4) we can combine the last two terms of the right-hand side of the expression and rewrite it as:

$$Y^T Y = \epsilon^T \epsilon + Y^T X (X^T X)^{-1} X^T Y \tag{B-5}$$

Total variation equals the residual variation plus that associated with the regression. In the case of Aitken estimates, R^2, as traditionally defined, has no clear meaning, since this partitioning is no longer possible [as in equation (B−3)].

Most econometrics texts suggest that Aitken estimation may be performed by first transforming the data prior to OLS regression (i.e., a positive definite matrix, Σ^{-1}, can be written as $W^T W$, where W is non-singular). The coefficient of determination defined in terms of the transformed data makes somewhat more sense, since these residuals, V, do allow for orthogonal partitioning.

$$V^T V = Y^T W^T W Y + \tag{B-6}$$

$$Y^T W^T W X (X^T W^T W X)^{-1} X^T W^T W X (X^T W^T W X)^{-1} X^T W^T W Y$$

$$- 2 Y^T W^T W X (X^T W^T W X)^{-1} X^T W^T W Y$$

Substituting for $W^T W$ we have:

$$Y^T \Sigma^{-1} Y = V^T V + Y^T \Sigma^{-1} X (X^T \Sigma^{-1} X)^{-1} X^T \Sigma^{-1} Y \tag{B-7}$$

While an R^2 calculated using the transformed data is bounded by zero and one, it does not [as a result of the term on the left in (B−7)] have an interpretation comparable to that of R^2 with OLS. This point is particularly important, since OLS computer routines used with transformed data will provide this R^2 as a measure of "goodness of fit." Equally important, calculation of R^2 using the GLS predictions and untransformed data does not allow for legitimate interpretation.

Bibliography

1. W.J. Baumol, *Economic Theory and Operations Analysis*, 3rd ed. Englewood Cliffs, N.J.: Prentice-Hall, Inc., 1972.

2. C.J. Cicchetti, J.J. Seneca, and P. Davidson, *The Demand and Supply of Outdoor Recreation*. New Brunswick, N.J.: Bureau of Economic Research, Rutgers University, 1969.

3. M. Clawson and Knetsch, *Economics of Outdoor Recreation*. Baltimore: Johns Hopkins University Press, 1966.

4. A.S. Goldberger, *Econometric Theory*. New York: John Wiley & Sons, 1964.

5. ————, *Topics in Regression Analysis*. New York: Macmillan, 1968.

6. S.M. Goldfeld and R.E. Quandt, *Nonlinear Methods in Econometrics*. Amsterdam: North Holland, 1972.

7. R. Gronau, *The Value of Time in Passenger Transportation: The Demand for Air Travel*. New York: Columbia University Press, 1970.

8. E.T. Haefele, ed. *The Governance of Common Property Resources*. Baltimore: Johns Hopkins University, 1974.

9. J. Johnston, *Econometric Methods*. 2nd ed. New York: McGraw-Hill, 1972.

10. J. Kmenta. *Elements of Econometrics*. New York: Macmillan, 1971.

11. J.V. Krutilla, ed. *Natural Environments: Studies in Theoretical and Applied Analysis*. Baltimore: Johns Hopkins University Press, 1972.

12. K.J. Lancaster, *Consumer Demand: A New Approach*. New York: Columbia University Press, 1971.

13. T.H. Naylor, ed. *The Design of Computer Simulation Experiments*. Durham, N.C.: Duke University Press, 1969.

14. H. Nikaido, *Introduction to Sets and Mappings in Modern Economics*. Amsterdam: North Holland, 1972.

15. V.K. Smith, *Monte Carlo Methods: Their Role for Econometrics*. Lexington, Mass.: Lexington Books, D.C. Heath, 1973.

16. ————, *Technical Change, Relative Prices and Environmental Resource Evaluation*. Baltimore: Johns Hopkins University Press, 1974.

17. V.K. Smith and J.V. Krutilla, *The Structure and Properties of a Wilderness Users Travel Simulator: With Special Application to the Spanish Peaks Area.* Baltimore: Johns Hopkins University Press, 1976.

18. H. Theil, *Principles of Econometrics.* New York: John Wiley & Sons, 1971.

Index

amenity services: concept of, 76, 78
Army Corps of Engineers Trinity
River Project, 6

Beck, .: consumer-as-producer, 15
Becker, G.S., 2; model of household
production, 7
Bob Marshall Wilderness, 20
Bohm, P., 22
Boundary Waters Canoe Area, 20
Bridger Wilderness, 20

Cicchetti, C.J.: personal attitudes on
congestion, 21; Fisher, A.C., and
Smith, V.K., 6; —, Seneca, J.J. and
Davidson, P., 5
Clawson, M., Knetsch, J.L.: travel-
cost approach, 22
congestion: consumer behavior model,
23; defined, 2; defined by attributes,
18; and encounter intensity, 64;
and price rationing, 81; quality
deterioration, 11
Conlisk, J. and Watts, H., 38
consumer: behavior, 3; characteristics,
28, 92; consumption and rate of
substitution, 70; and demography
variables, 29; Lancaster model, 24;
lifestyle, 2; socioeconomic variables,
30
costs: and benefit stream, 68; congestion argument, 14; congestion
and willingness-to-pay function, 29;
ecological, 80; function and concept,
4; methodology of analysis, 11; and
shadow price, 18; travel costs in
analysis, 48

decisionmaking: and encounter
intensity, 72, 73; preservation/
development, 67; resource allocation, 13; use intensity, 70

encounters: intensity, 63; and socioeconomic variables, 92, 93; types of
and scale, 21; and use relationship,
72; variables and intensity, 30;
variables and methodology, 50
externalities, defined, 1

Fisher, A.C. and Krutilla, J.V., 92;
— and Cicchetti, C.J., 76

Goldfeld, S.M. and Quandt, R.E., 61

Haveman, R.H., 11
heteroscedasticity, 48, 58
High Uintas Primitive Area, 20
homoscedasticity, 44

income elasticity, 5
interaction: user, 3

Kmenta, J., 60
Krutilla, J.V.-Cicchetti, C.J.: model,
8, 68, 94

Lancaster, K.J., 17; model, 19
Lucas, Robert, 41, 93

management: and resource allocation,
3; and service production, 13
measurement: aggregate congestion
costs, 13; congestion, 11; Kuhn-
Tucker conditions, 17; and nontime-

About the Authors

Charles J. Cicchetti is the Director of Wisconsin's Office of Emergency Energy Assistance on leave from the University of Wisconsin at Madison, where he is an Associate Professor of Economics. He received his undergraduate training at Colorado College and his Ph.D. from Rutgers University. Between 1969 and 1972 he was a Research Associate at Resources for the Future in Washington, D.C. He has published books on forecasting the demand for outdoor recreation, the Alaska Pipeline, and the problems of regulating the electric power industry.

V. Kerry Smith is a Professor of Economics at the State University of New York at Binghamton. He received his B.A. and Ph.D. from Rutgers University. He has served as an Assistant and Associate Professor of Statistics at Bowling Green State University and a Research Associate at Resources for the Future in Washington, D.C. His previous research includes books on Monte Carlo Methods and the effects of technical change on the relative prices of the amenities from natural environments.